A PLACE TO TAKE ROOT

A PLACE TO TAKE ROOT

A Memoir of Becoming *Sure*
as an International Student

YUJIN KIM

NEW DEGREE PRESS

COPYRIGHT © 2022 YUJIN KIM

All rights reserved.

A PLACE TO TAKE ROOT

A MEMOIR OF BECOMING SURE AS AN INTERNATIONAL STUDENT

ISBN

979-8-88504-149-2   *Paperback*
979-8-88504-782-1   *Kindle Ebook*
979-8-88504-261-1   *Digital Ebook*

To all newcomers

CONTENTS

INTRODUCTION 11

PART 1   HONEYMOON

Chapter 1   **LONGING**
All the Great Things Happen in America   19

Chapter 2   **SKY**
The Two Faces of Self-Doubt   25

Chapter 3   **MAGIC**
Some Wishes Come True
When We Least Expect Them   35

PART 2   A BUMP ON THE ROAD

Chapter 4   **SQUINTING**
Broken—That Was What My Broken
English Made Me Feel   53

Chapter 5   **STOPOVERS**
Everywhere Is Somewhere I Stop By   63

Chapter 6   **SECRET BOX**
When Diversity Expands or Shrinks Us   73

Chapter 7	**BABY ADULT**		
	Learning to Live on My Own Terms	83	
Chapter 8	**PERFECT OR NOT**		
	Seeing Forest beyond the Trees	97	

PART 3   RECOVERY

Chapter 9	**FIT IN OR LET IN**	
	Rooted in Myself	107
Chapter 10	**SAFETY NET**	
	Rooted in Us	117
Chapter 11	**REAL OPTIMISM**	
	Rooted in Truth	127

PART 4   MASTERY

Chapter 12	**RENEWED**	
	Would I Still Come to America?	145

A BRIEF GUIDE ON BECOMING SURE   151

APPENDIX   157

ACKNOWLEDGMENTS   161

INTRODUCTION

On a cold day in Boston in 2016, I was waiting for the train after my classes at Boston University. I was listening to one of my favorite songs, "Viva La Vida" by Coldplay. With its title translated into "Long Live Life," I used to think the song was about winning and felt empowered by it. I listened to it whenever I worked toward my goals—whether that was for the Korean college entrance exam or coming to America.

Because my English became better in America, I realized the song was not about winning. It was about a fallen king looking back on his glorious days—the days when bells were ringing and choirs were singing for him. The king's life had much changed since, and he now slept alone and swept streets he used to own.

How ironic, I thought.

Freedom and opportunities. These were the reasons why I came to America. I worked hard to come to this country, spending over a third of my life studying English. My excitement, however, overshadowed the darker side of moving to a new country. In America, I was dealing with struggles that weren't obvious to an outsider, like the king from "Viva La Vida."

The train arrived, and I slowly walked into it. I sat down on a window seat in a half-full train and looked outside the window. All I could see was the reflection of my face as the train passed through a dark tunnel. My reflection wore her hood up with her headset on, blocking the energy of the city. She seemed tired and lost.

Looking at my reflection, my head was full of question marks. What do I have on my resume? Would people care whether I went to one of the most privileged universities in Korea? Would I be able to get a job here after graduation? In people's eyes, like the man on a bike yelling at me in Chinese, I'm just a shy Asian girl. Could I ever make real friends here?

I now know all these question marks were the signs that I was *unsure*. I can't pinpoint exactly what, but it felt like an overall state of mind affecting my life and everything around me.

This feeling of being unsure manifested itself in many ways. I felt like an imposter, who thought I was not good enough despite my past success. I became self-conscious about my English to the point where I had to repeat what I was about to say over and over in my head. I used to be an extroverted and confident person but started worrying about whether I fit in with the people around me. I felt incompetent but was paralyzed by my own perfectionism. Once I started feeling unsure about everything, my self-esteem plummeted.

Now six years have passed since I first arrived in the United States in 2016. Many people, places, and events provided answers to the countless questions I had. As I turned each of my question marks into a period or even an exclamation point, I became surer. This doesn't mean I don't have any difficulties, but I am sure about my ability to tackle them with a sense of conviction, optimism, and willingness to be vulnerable.

A Place to Take Root is a portrait of the lessons I learned in the past six years on becoming sure—as an international student, and more broadly, as someone living in a new country.

The memoir is split into four parts: Honeymoon, Crisis, Recovery, and Mastery.[1] These are four stages of cultural adjustment people go through when moving to a new country, as research shows.

Part I. Honeymoon is a background story about my younger years in South Korea and how that affected my decision to come to America.

Part II. A Bump on the Road revolves around five mental health challenges commonly experienced among international students and immigrants: Language and communication insecurity, feeling of otherness, stereotyping, feeling of being incompetent, and perfectionism. Later, I understood they reinforce the cycle of feeling unsure or self-doubt, and I delve into how I overcame each of them.

Part III. Recovery presents three broader lessons I learned on becoming sure. In a nutshell, we should keep our roots in three places to become sure: in ourselves, in our "safety net," and in the reality. I tell stories about how I learned these lessons and why they are important for managing self-doubt and safeguarding our self-esteem.

Part IV. Mastery presents who I am now and reflects on an important question I was afraid to answer ever since I

---

[1] Lysgaard (1955) shows that in the *Honeymoon* stage, we look forward to our experience in the new country with the sense of excitement that may overshadow our worries. As we settle down, we face challenges, with some experiencing homesickness and isolation, entering the *Crisis* stage. During the *Recovery* stage, we interact frequently with locals, improving our understanding of the culture and language. When we arrive in the *Mastery* phase, we feel a renewed sense of identity, which reflects our experience at home and in America, feeling accepted and ready for the next journey.

came to America: Would I still come to America if I knew what it would be like?

Finally, I summarize my lessons in the last chapter, *A Brief Guide on Becoming Sure*.

The memoir is largely chronological, but I sometimes refer to an event that happened further in the future. This is because each chapter has its own theme, and I'm tying a series of related events that happened in different times. That said, I made sure to note the timeline so you can follow along with the stories smoothly.

You may be one of the million international students living in America, immigrants, expatriates, or none of these. Whatever category you find yourself in, we all deal with changes in our environments and feel inadequate from time to time. I wish that this book can help you navigate your change and become surer—about yourself and everything else you care about.

As you finish the memoir, I wish you to take time reflecting some of your big changes in life and how they have affected your mental health and personal growth. I would love to hear whether my lessons have resonated with you and helped you process some of the challenging yet courageous times of your life.

As a memoir, this book reflects my present recollections of experiences as truthfully as possible.

It is based on true stories with actual people, places, and events, but some names and characteristics have been changed to protect the privacy of people.

1

HONEYMOON

CHAPTER 1

LONGING

All the Great Things Happen in America

On every New Year's Eve, my dad would bring my sister and me to a temple on the nearby mountain. Wintertime in Korea is freezing cold, but we still went to the temple wearing two pairs of gloves, two pairs of socks, and multiple layers of clothes. More than hundreds of people would gather at the temple—lining up to ring the giant bell and making their wishes for the new year.[2] After that, people would write their wishes on paper and throw them away into a big fire pit. I loved our tradition and never complained about how cold it was, even when the weather numbed my face.

In 2009, I wrote the wish to go to America on my paper as a sixteen-year-old high school student. At that time, this wish seemed too big to come true. My family lived in a small town in a rural area of Korea, and I only knew one person who studied in America. But this is what we do on New

---

2   New Year's Day is special for every Korean because we have our own age counting system where everyone gets a year older on that day.

Year's Eve: We make the wishes that scare us. I hesitantly yet carefully wrote my words on the paper and threw it in the fire pit. I stood in front of the fire, watching my paper ascending to the sky.

* * *

My family—Mom, Dad, my younger sister, Yenny, and my furry brother, Sia—lived in Cheon-An, which is one and a half hours away from Seoul by car. Though Cheon-An is a quite big city that serves as the hub connecting the rest of the country, my town was in the countryside surrounded by a mountain. The folklore says a spirit lives in the mountain bringing lucks and comforts to everyone in the town.

Because my home was tucked away in the countryside, it took me forty minutes to an hour to get to school by bus. The commute was especially difficult because I would go to my middle school before my teachers so I didn't get caught for my long hair. At school, we were told to keep our hair within four inches below the shoulder line and only wear a school uniform slightly larger than our bodies to cover our silhouette. We were supposed to have straight hair, even if we were born with curly hair. We were not allowed to wear colorful jackets or shoes, and if a student did, a teacher would confiscate those clothes.

Why? We need to focus on one goal: *study hard* so we could present ourselves however we wanted to in college. But I loved my long hair and all my colorful hoodies and sneakers. To avoid getting caught, I used a few strategies by going to school early or disguising my long hair with a low bun. But whenever I was relaxed with my hair, that was when teachers noticed it. I frequently got called with other girls with long and curly hair. We would then get all sorts of punishment—from kneeling down on the floor to running a mile-long track five times.

Every time I got caught, it wasn't fully explained why these behaviors were bad. They said these were distractions to our goal of going to a prestigious university. To prove them wrong, I made a point of staying within the top 5 percent of the class, but that didn't stop them from enforcing the rules. Eventually, it got to the point when the teacher called my mom to school because I refused to get a haircut.

Then I became angry. When a teacher told me I should not wear my red hoodie, I questioned, "Why? You did not pay for it." When a teacher told me I should get a haircut by next week, I said, "Why? We don't use our hair to study." I was mad at the regulations and punishment, but I was madder at the reasoning behind it. I couldn't link these measures to any meaningful causes. In my eyes, they were there to thwart individualism and to raise docile individuals who can conform. My anger became worse with puberty and spilled over to other areas of life. I hung out with my friends doing what we weren't supposed to do, didn't pick up my parents' calls, and missed school to do karaoke instead.[3]

These behaviors did not endear me to many of the teachers, and our relationships soured. One time, a gym teacher caught me and two other friends at the back entrance while

---

3   Early on, my mom taught me it was okay to speak up and stand up for myself. There was one time in my elementary school I walked away from the classroom because the whole class got a group punishment for someone's missing shoes. I was afraid she would scold me, but instead, she told me, "You are someone who can stand up for yourself." She still wonders whether she should have scolded me, and that would have made me a happy teenager. But I can assure her she did the right thing because her validating my choice made me value independence and individuality.

sneaking back into school. We didn't foresee he would stand right there to catch us. After coming from karaoke, we smelled like cigarettes, our hair was long, and we wore brand hoodies. He made us follow him to a dark storage room where he stocked up the materials for his gym classes. He told us to get in a plank position and hit us with a mop. Each time the mop hit our butts, we fell to the floor only to get back up. The next day, we had purple bruises all over our thighs, just high enough that our skirts could cover them. But none of us cried. Instead, we laughed it out because that's how we coped with our anger and frustration. My friends and I were stubbornly holding onto self-expression, even when that hurt us.

* * *

My high school had similar rules as my middle school, and the hide-and-seek between me and teachers continued. Then there was my friend Hannah, who understood my frustration but dealt with it differently. Hannah lived with her aunt in Los Angeles, who owned a successful Korean restaurant while the rest of her family lived in Korea. Her aunt's house, according to the pictures she showed me, was a two-story house with a pool, a garage, and ample space.

She came back to Korea after finishing middle school in Los Angeles. She could have lived longer there, but her family thought it would be easier to get into college in Korea if she had some Korean education. They regretted this decision later, though. Many Korean universities did offer a special type of admission to students who studied abroad for at least three years, but that had to include one year in high school. Since she came back before high school, she wasn't eligible for this special admission and had to take the Korean college entrance exam like any other student.

Even though Hannah also grappled with the legitimacy of the rules, she kept her hair short and wore discrete clothes. She understood how important it was to have positive assessments from teachers in her college admission. I didn't like how calculated that was, but I knew she would eventually get what she wanted with a little sacrifice.

I asked Hannah a lot of questions about America. Hannah said all sorts of people, things, and opportunities exist there. Being one of the largest countries in the world, people fly over seven hours to cross the country from one end to the other. Some Americans eat bread as frequently as we eat rice and *kimchi*. America is called "a melting pot" because people came from all over the world and their cultures coexist and influence each other. It seemed different from my country, where it takes fewer than ten hours by car from one end to the other and people are ethnically and culturally similar. "Look at New York and San Francisco," she once said. "All the great things happen in America."

With nostalgia, she told me how she used to get out of school at two in America compared to nine in the evening now; that was more than twelve hours at school. She showed me some pictures of her middle school with her hair going far below her chest wearing pink Nike hoodies. Many of her friends in the pictures were also Koreans; most of them were tan and wore different hairstyles and outfits.

America sounded like a paradise for high school students—a place where students can do anything with their hair and clothes! A place where students don't need to stay until nine in the evening! It was incredibly liberating to see how free they looked; I wondered if I could ever have that.

Despite my troubling puberty, I dreamed of being a successful career woman who worked across borders and helped others. America sounded like a perfect place to practice English, meet people from different walks of life, and start a career on the global stage—all while enjoying freedom and abundance. In the end, there should be a reason why rich Koreans send their kids to America. People pay more than $25,000 as "birth tourists" to get their kids American citizenship, risking their safety and comfort as pregnant women. Why would people try so hard to get there if it does not give them better lives?

I knew that going to America was extremely costly and competitive. Usually, people send their children to an American university, but that was not an option for my family. I could go to a graduate school in America because a government scholarship was available. Or I could get a job in an American company based in Korea and then transfer to the American office. But I also knew that all these require tremendous luck—to the point that some people are willing to fly to America with a travel visa, make under-the-table money, and hope they can one day be legal immigrants.

For some reason, though, America felt like a mountain I could climb—a challenging one, but one within my reach. I felt like I deserved it—to live in a land where people enjoy freedom and opportunities. I started longing for the country that I'd never even been to and couldn't wait to be the person I would become in America.

CHAPTER 2

SKY

The Two Faces of Self-Doubt

I had two math teachers in high school: Mr. Kim and Mr. Park. Even though they both taught math, Mr. Kim was more of a pessimist while Mr. Park was an optimist. Mr. Kim watered a seed of self-doubt in me, while Mr. Park taught me how to persevere despite self-doubt. I was influenced by both of them—I had strong self-doubt but also strived for my goals.

"Don't think you can make it into SKY," Mr. Kim told in class. "Our school isn't good enough." At the time, he said other private high schools, like the International Baccalaureate, follow a curriculum designed just for the SKY. Our school was in a small city, so it would be hard for most of us to compete with the rich and connected in Seoul.

SKY is the Korean equivalent of the Ivy League. It stands for three top universities: Seoul National University, Korea University, and Yonsei University. Many Koreans believe that SKY can get people far in their careers and help them achieve higher social status. Just look at who graduated from these schools: former presidents, lawyers, physicians, CEOs, athletes, and even celebrities. Even though it is debatable how much the SKY education itself contributes to the success of the students, a SKY degree works like a passport, proving the student's intelligence and work ethic.

To get into the SKY, students must have near-to-perfect scores in all subjects of the Korean national entrance exam, *Suneung*. *Suneung* includes the Korean language, mathematics, English, and two electives like Korean history and philosophy. Even the slightest mishap during the exam could be a deal-breaker for college admission, so the exam needs to be perfectly fair and free of errors. Testing takes place across the country once a year in November; airplanes don't even fly during the listening tests to prevent noises.

Suneung is important to many Koreans because it *is* a step on the ladder to SKY. Except for some students with international backgrounds, *Suneung* is usually the most important criterion for college admission.[4] Because all students have resources for *Suneung* at school and the government-owned education channel, it was theoretically possible for any student to excel in this exam.[5] Thus, *Suneung* is a big deal for most high school students and their parents, whether rich or not.

With that said, having a non-SKY degree can be disadvantageous. For example, chances are often high that a

---

[4] As I mentioned in Chapter 1 briefly, many Korean universities offer a special admission for students who finished at least three years of education abroad. Students applying to college this way do not need to take *Suneung*.

[5] This is called EBS. EBS offers high-quality lessons for all *Suneung* subjects for free. It also produces study materials for *Suneung*, and some of *Suneung* questions are adopted from EBS study materials. This is a way for the government to close the resource gaps among students by encouraging them to use free resources instead of expensive private tutoring.

company prefers candidates from the SKY even when they may have less experience than applicants with a non-SKY degree. This unspoken yet clear favoritism had contributed to overly heated competition among high school students and their parents. The government eventually enacted a "blind hiring" law in 2017 that all public enterprises must not ask applicants which school they graduated from.

Even though I didn't endorse the elitism or the end-all-be-all approach to college admission, I wanted to experience what it would be like to study at one of these prestigious universities. I knew that a SKY degree would give me the advantage I needed to go study in America. To me, SKY was about exploring the world outside the smallness of my apartment, my town, and my country. It was about rising above the system, bringing a better life for myself and my family, and eventually influencing society.

"Don't get your hopes too high," Mr. Kim would say. His words got me thinking, *What's the point of studying for hours if it won't pay off at all? Why is he bothering to teach us anything if he doesn't believe we can succeed?* I remember sitting in class and feeling frustrated at his words. I ended up bursting into tears, but I hid my face so no one noticed.

The thing is I doubted myself too. SKY *is* an ambitious goal. It is reserved for the top 1 percent of all students nationally. In my school, only a handful of students had a fighting chance for the SKY. But none of these students were like me. They were already in the top 1 percent. They had the best relationships with teachers. Some of them had international backgrounds with their parents being professors and doctors graduating from the SKY.

But people make it into the SKY even when they didn't start from the top. Why not me?

After a ten-minute break, Mr. Park came into the classroom. He believed that anyone could learn and become good at math. He would wake up a sleeping student and stay after the class answering any questions. He never gave up on his students, even if they called themselves a math failure. Mr. Park often told us persistence could bring us anywhere, even to SKY.

When he entered the classroom, he saw my tearful face and asked me what happened. I didn't say anything at first, but he noticed how upset I was and asked again. I told him what Mr. Kim said and how I already felt like a huge failure.

His face slightly turned red with anger. He said, "Remember, persistence can get you anywhere."

After that day, I despised cynics and made a point of only listening to optimistic people—my parents, Mr. Park, and my friends. Still, I internalized these doubts that became a nagging voice in my head. When the voice whispered, "I'm doing this wrong" or "I won't make it," I brushed off the voice and studied harder. I was walking, studying, and sleeping with a big knot of anxiety in my stomach but didn't try to detangle it. If I faced it, it would eat me alive.

This knot became a big distraction, and it didn't lead to the results I wanted in my first *Suneung*.

At the graduation ceremony, students who got into SKY were recognized. They were called to the stage and received a trophy for their success; Hannah was one of them. I watched them from my chair and hoped no one would ask me which school I got into. No one said a word about my failure, but I felt like someone was telling me, "I told you. SKY is too ambitious."

* * *

It was my dad who pulled me out of the disappointment from my first *Suneung*. I initially told my parents I would not go to college at all and take the test again. I did not like plan B; if I was going to reach for the stars, I preferred to jump for the stars even though I was standing on the edge of a cliff. Having a plan B only reinforced my doubt that my plan A may not succeed.

My father's mind worked differently. He did not like to stretch himself too thin. He believed in using a parachute if you have to jump for the stars. He said, "Just apply for a couple of universities in Seoul. If you get in, you can decide whether or not to accept the offer." He explained that having an option was not about doubting ourselves; it was about knowing what we can and cannot control and preparing for the less-than-ideal situation.

That night, my application went out to two universities. One of them was Sookmyung Women's University, which became my first university.

Soon after graduating from high school, I moved to Seoul to attend Sookmyung Women's University. Seoul was hectic and large for a nineteen-year-old girl who grew up in a small town, but I didn't feel out of place. I loved what the city could offer: bars, restaurants, karaoke, and clothing shops. The abundance of things, people, and places overwhelmed and energized me at the same time. Luckily for me, I didn't meet any sassy locals, the old stereotype of Seoul residents.

At SWU, I had a squad of five women who shared little secrets about our relationships, went to a bar on Fridays, and made a trip together to Yangpyung, a remote town surrounded by a mountain. My favorite moments with them were when we sat together on a school bench between classes, which made me feel like I belonged in their company. On top of all these new and exciting memories, I relished my newfound freedom to do as I pleased with my hair and clothes.

Over time, I realized that going to SKY was not the end all be all, and there was much to enjoy in life outside of school. I loved spending time with my squad. I was exposed to people from all walks of life and learned different subjects. But I promised myself I would retake the test in the next testing period. I wanted to know what SKY could offer and to give it a try one last time.

* * *

After one semester at SWU, I took a semester off and moved back home. I studied at a small and quiet public library. Every morning, I listened to Coldplay's "Viva La Vida." Hoping that the song could help me win this game, I put it on repeat and listened to it when walking to the library. *You got this. You will win.* The song made it easier for me to repeat these lines to myself.

My life was simple. Every day, I walked to the library by seven in the morning. At noon, Mom dropped off lunch. After lunch, I started studying again until 6 p.m. Then I walked back home with my sister, ate dinner, watched an episode of a Korean show, and continued studying until 11 p.m. Every weekend was a hike day with my father, and as a post-hike meal, we had a bowl of *jjajangmyun* and *jjambbong*, black bean noodles and spicy seafood noodles. It was easy to work on my goal because I was surrounded by people who believed in me.

Unlike my first *Suneung*, I used my doubt to find a solution. I learned from my dad that my doubts can signal that I should be clearer on what I can and cannot control. Whenever

I thought, *What if I won't get in?*, I would talk to different people and learn about their experiences and study tips. This gave me confidence I was going in the right direction.

Some of my worries didn't have an answer; they were just the normal nerves from preparing for the big exam. To keep this emotion from becoming a distraction, I visualized myself acing the test—like an athlete preparing for a big game. I visualized myself stepping into the testing place, sitting down, tackling the problems easily and quickly until I fell asleep. At some point, I was *sure* I would win because I could *see* it clearly.

* * *

The time passed rapidly, and soon it was the *Suneung* day.

I was assigned to take my second *Suneung* in a middle school about forty minutes away by car. My mother and I headed to the testing site together in a taxi because the government encouraged people to take a cab to reduce traffic and prevent students from being late for the test. Sitting behind the driver's seat, I listened to "Viva La Vida" one last time before taking the test. I looked at my mom in the passenger seat. Her body was slightly turned toward me, as if she was telling me, "I am with you, I protect you, and I support you." When I got out of the taxi, she stepped out and gave me a warm, firm hug.

I stepped into the classroom and found my seat on the far left side. This was good because no one was on my left; no one would distract me, as I was right handed. My desk and chair felt stable and fit for my height. The student behind me also looked closely into his surroundings. He even asked me politely if I had a habit of fidgeting my leg to make sure he didn't have any distractions. I said I didn't.

Once the exam started at nine, my mind knew exactly how to tackle each question with calmness and confidence. I wasn't surprised if I didn't know the answer to a question; I had already trained myself to know how to react. During lunchtime, I ate my favorite beef and radish soup my mom had made. By five o'clock, I stepped out of the classroom and closed the sliding door behind me knowing *I had killed it.*

When I got home, I ran to the computer to check the answers. The English test was one of the most difficult ones in *Suneung* history, and I got all the answers right. Both of my electives, Korean history and philosophy, were also a hundred percent. I missed three questions in Korean and one question in mathematics. In the entire exam, I only had four incorrect answers.

I knew this wouldn't guarantee my admission to SKY, but it was certainly within my reach. I applied to six universities including Korea University and Yonsei University. I knew my chances for getting accepted to these schools were higher than others because they had writing tests I was fairly confident about.

A few months later, I started getting emails from these schools. Five of them were rejections. I still thought something would happen for me with Korea University for a reason I cannot explain.

After five months from *Suneung*, I got an email from Korea University. I looked up my application number and hit enter.

"Here we go," I said in a low voice.

Two seconds later, a welcome message popped up on the screen.

Congratulations on your admission to Korea University.

We're delighted to have you as our student.

I sat there feeling my heart soaring. I couldn't believe I got in. I got into a school that accepts fewer than 1 percent of applicants. It was my school, and no one could tell me otherwise. Setting a big goal and achieving it as a teenager showed that while I may doubt myself, I could use that doubt to my advantage.

My dad celebrates happy occasions with a nice plate of *sashimi*, so that night, he bought a big plate of *sashimi* and *soju*, Korean liquor. My mother told me, "I'm so proud of you," again and again. Yenny kept telling me she was so proud to have me as her sister. I called Mr. Park and some of the other teachers who encouraged me throughout high school and said, "Look, I got into Korea University!"

CHAPTER 3

MAGIC

Some Wishes Come True When We Least Expect Them

When I got into Korea University, I felt like a magician who could make anything happen; but I quickly realized I had no control over how my magic worked.

Korea University had everything I could ask for as a college student. A beautiful and spacious campus with well-maintained trees and grass. Smart, driven, and energetic students who care about their communities and society. Philosophical discussions that we could barely understand yet always taught us something new. An abundance of student activities and learning opportunities. Ethnic and national diversity among students and professors. Reputation in the world of academics, politics, and businesses. It was truly a bridge to the rest of the world.

In the fall semester of my second year, I joined a volunteer group that helped exchange students from abroad.[6]

---

6 Universities in Korea start their academic years in March. The first or spring semester lasts from March to June, and the second or fall semester is from September to December.

There, I met Eli from Boston. She was a tall girl with big brown eyes who seemed to be able to convince anybody to believe what she says. Her parents came to the United States during the Cambodian genocide, Khmer Rouge. Living in a rough neighborhood in Boston, she was exposed to school violence and racial discrimination as a teenager. Many of her friends had kids before they became adults; others were in jail.

Even if she grew up surrounded by a sense of failure, she had the ambition to become a successful business owner. Eli believed anything was possible. She liked to say "I will figure it out" even though I didn't see the way out. It was as if she needed to guard her dream from other people. We were both attracted to each other's ambitions and used to joke about who would become a millionaire first.

Eli was the East Coast version of Hannah and would tell me what it was like to live in America. Unlike Hannah, though, her description of America was not entirely rosy. She told me about substance abuse and gun violence that happened in the neighborhood she grew up in. She talked about the poverty she experienced as a child, living with parents and a grandmother on food stamps, and how badly she wanted a pair of Nike sneakers in her elementary school. The contrast between Hannah and Eli's worlds put a spotlight on inequality in America. Still, Eli was hopeful she could find a way out. Her optimism attracted me to America even more.

We often went to a Korean pub named An-Am-Street that had our favorite coffee-flavored beer. That night, we were talking over our drinks and snacks. I talked to her about how much I wanted to go to America. She told me about a friend from China who transferred to her university. At this point, I couldn't afford college tuition fees in America, which was five times more expensive than what my parents were paying now to study at Korea University. Plus, I worked too hard to get into Korea University and loved my school. I wondered if it was worth it to go all the way to America when I could just stay here.

"If that's what you really want, you'll find a way," she said.

That night, I went back home and sat down with my laptop. Her way of thinking started to brush off on me. Until now, I had been waiting for the right time to go to America. Maybe after college. Maybe when I get a job. But maybe, there might be a way. I started looking for opportunities to go to America earlier, murmuring Eli's magic words, *I will find a way.*

After thirty minutes or so, I found an advertisement about an education program for Korean and American students. Over three weeks, students would travel to California, Indiana, Washington, DC, and New York City. I checked all the boxes for who they considered to be eligible for the program, so I submitted an application. I went through the interview a few months later and got selected for the program—even with my limited English. I sometimes wondered if I would have gotten this opportunity if I didn't have Korea University under my belt.

Eli's magic words worked wonders. I was now participating in this program during the next summer break of my third year at Korea University. I also raised the participation fees from the university who in exchange only requested a report documenting my experience. After this program, I went to the University of British Columbia (UBC) in Canada as an exchange student. I even got a scholarship of $7,000 from a large Korean foundation for my living expenses in Canada. At this point, what I wrote down on my paper on New Year's Eve no longer needed to be a secret. I could share my dream to anyone, and they would say I could do it. Everything I wished for was within my reach.

When the trip became official, my mom and I went to an outlet mall. She got me a couple of dresses, blazers, blouses, and skirts to wear at the conference. It made me feel bad that my mom spent almost $1,000 on clothes, but I knew she wanted to do that. She knew I was once a frustrated and angry as a teenager who could not wait to live in a bigger world. She had dropped off my lunch every day at the library while working overnight. She took care of me since day one. I couldn't wait to give back to her because we earned this together.

* * *

I arrived in San Francisco that summer. Like my two years in Seoul, the entire summer was blurred by my excitement. I was overwhelmed by the gold lights of San Francisco. In Sacramento, I shook hands with the first Korean-born American woman to serve as the US representative for California. In New York City, some locals were kind enough to help me and my friends find some Shake Shack burgers, which we heard were a must-try in New York.[7] In Indiana, the night sky was navy blue; I often took a walk at night to see the moon. Because we could only see one side of the moon, it was comforting to know what I saw in this country was what my family would see in Korea.

I loved how big, diverse, and dynamic America was. I wanted to come back to America after my exchange program in Canada. Before I headed to Canada, I visited Eli in Boston and asked her to bring me to some campuses, including Boston

---

7   Shake Shack is now available in Korea, but it was not back then in 2016.

University, which I had heard of. I saw quite a few international students walking across the beautiful buildings alongside Commonwealth Avenue. If Korea University can afford me all these opportunities, what more would I have here?

I can see myself here; I want to be here, I thought while passing by the BU campus.

Eli then brought up the story of her friend who transferred from China as an international student. She also mentioned her roommate was moving out after graduating, so if I ever decided to move, I could live with her.

At the end of the summer, I came to Vancouver and studied there for a semester. Tucked away at the far left side of Vancouver surrounded by the ocean, the campus, foliage, and sunset made me feel as if I was living in a movie. I lived on the eighth floor of a dormitory building and loved looking outside every morning, feeling grateful to be there.

Classroom environments were also different than what I had at Korea University. I felt like more resources were there: Professors had regular office hours and were more approachable, homework was an important component of your grade alongside exams, classes were interactive, and a lot of students exchanged their thoughts freely. I didn't need to memorize every detail to excel in the exams. Instead, I had to really understand key concepts and be able to explain them. These learning styles suit me as someone who learns better in interactive and hands-on environments.

My experience at the UBC pushed me to consider transferring to an American university. But this was such a hard decision for a twenty-two-year-old. If I left for America, I would leave behind my family and my university, the SKY that I worked extremely hard for. I didn't plan to ask my parents for the tuition fees because I learned that international students could take private loans with a cosigner. Still, I would need their help with other expenses. Things would be also uncertain in America; how would I know if I would become successful there?

However, I didn't know if a Korean education would help me with my career goals. My main goal was to work at an international organization. For that, I needed to improve my English, have more experience with diversity, and learn tangible skills to be useful at an international organization. I only had two years left at Korea University and doubted I would get the needed experience there. The more I thought about it, the more it made sense to go to America.

After coming back to Korea from Canada, I decided to apply to Boston University. Honestly, there was no strong reason why I chose BU. It was a no-brainer that I wanted to go to Massachusetts to stay closer to Eli. I knew the school had a good reputation in and out of the US. I had also seen the school in person and how diverse it was. I only applied for that school; I was gambling in a sense. I would rather have the faith decide for me; if I didn't get in, that would mean I should stay at Korea University.

This was the first time my ambition scared my parents, even though they were supportive. My dad took it especially hard. The night I brought up the idea, my dad drank alone in the kitchen. I could understand what was hurting him. He thought it was too risky to get a whole year off to study for *Suneung*. Now his daughter was saying she would be transferring to an American school, leaving behind what she worked extremely hard for.

Being starry-eyed, I was busy assuring them everything would be okay rather than thinking through the process. I didn't want to give them any reason to stop me. When they talked about their concerns including the tuition fees, I repeated the magic words, "Don't worry. I will find a way"—not knowing what I would actually be going to do.

Then I got accepted to BU. I was elated; my dream was happening a lot quicker than I had ever imagined. At the same time, I was not completely sure whether this would be a good decision. I learned how to use my doubts as a signal to be clear on the problems I can control. However, I was too desperate and impatient to even think about what problems I would be dealing with. I was clear on what I wanted, and that was all that mattered. I would figure everything out on the fly.

* * *

As soon as I got accepted to BU, I had to sort out my visa, which would grant permission to stay in the United States. I read and studied any information about getting a student visa. The interview would be in English, and while chances were high to get a student visa, I wanted to make sure I didn't mess up. The practice took most of my time in Korea, so my family and I didn't spend much time with each other.

Practice after practice.

Prayer after prayer.

That was how I spent the last few weeks before my interview.

Based on my research, people are asked questions about their career goals and plans after studying in the States. When they deemed we would be harmless to the country *and* don't have the intention to migrate to the US, we may earn the visa or may not. I had some good answers for the interview, especially regarding my career plans. Since I was a child, working at an international organization was all I wanted. And that would be my answer; I am going to study economics at BU and hope to work at an international organization afterward.

My appointment was early in the morning at ten, so my mom got me a ticket for a high-speed train that halved my travel time to Seoul.

"Don't worry. I can handle it myself," I assured Mom when she asked me if I wanted her to come with me.

It was a cold morning when I arrived at the US embassy. Over twenty people waited in front of the building, surrounded by the American flags and security officers. The building looked nothing like American. Rather, it was a concrete building that reminded me of North Korea.

I overheard the conversation between the couple standing next to me. They worked at Google, but their visa had almost expired. To continue working there, they had to come back to Korea and sort out the issue. Everyone here was talented and fortunate enough to get accepted by some American company or school, and we were about to test our luck one more time.

I walked into the building, which looked as rigid as its interior. It looked like a typical motor vehicle registry, with only low voices and typing noises. I waited after checking in, trying to be as nice as possible to everyone I bumped into. Even though I knew exactly what I was going to say, I was nervous about the unknown.

My number showed up on the screen, and I walked up to the desk. I sat down and greeted the interviewer in Korean. My interviewer seemed to be Korean, but he spoke English.

After asking a couple of questions, he looked at me and my paperwork. I didn't know what he was thinking, and it was hard to read his face. Then he asked me where I was planning to go after graduation. I knew it was an important question because the question was to gauge whether I had any intention of moving to the States.

"I'll work at an international organization."

The interviewer looked at me again and took a picture of me. "You are all set," he said.

Now it was official; I was going to America *and* had the right to do so.

A few weeks after, everyone except Sia, my furry brother, saw me off at the airport. Sia was home because we weren't sure whether we could bring him to the airport. But the night before, Sia slept with me as if he knew I was going somewhere far away. When we were leaving the house, Sia wagged his tail at the door as though he was telling us to bring him with us. I gave him a big hug and said, "I love you, and I am sorry that I can't bring you."

Every time I traveled, it was hard to leave my family behind. There was not a single time I did not cry at the airport. There was not a single time I wished I could stay longer here with my family. But somehow, I knew I was meant to go to America, the big world. I knew my parents also wanted to see me fly high, and America was the country that could incubate my ambition and turn it into reality.

"I'll call you," I said in front of the gate.

My mom gave me a big hug like she did when she saw me off on the *Suneung* day. My father patted my back. Yenny waved at me as if she was telling me, "I got you. Don't worry about here." *I count on you to keep them company*, I thought, watching her smile.

I started walking toward the gate. My family was still there, watching me walking through the door. As I scanned my boarding pass, I was struck by a thought: *When would I see them again?* but I gave them a big smile. As soon as I crossed the gate, I let myself cry.

Waiting to board, I looked around the waiting area. Many people seemed to be students. Now that I got what I wanted, I kept looking back at what I left behind in Korea: my family, my friends, and my school. I wondered why so many Koreans go to America. Are things *really* better there? I kept repeating to myself that I will find a way, but my self-doubt started to rise. I knew that ignoring the negative talk only makes it louder, but I was too scared to face it head on. If this turned out to be a bad decision, I wasn't sure I could live with it.

Walking Sia in my hometown

Sia "protecting" me while I was studying for Suneung

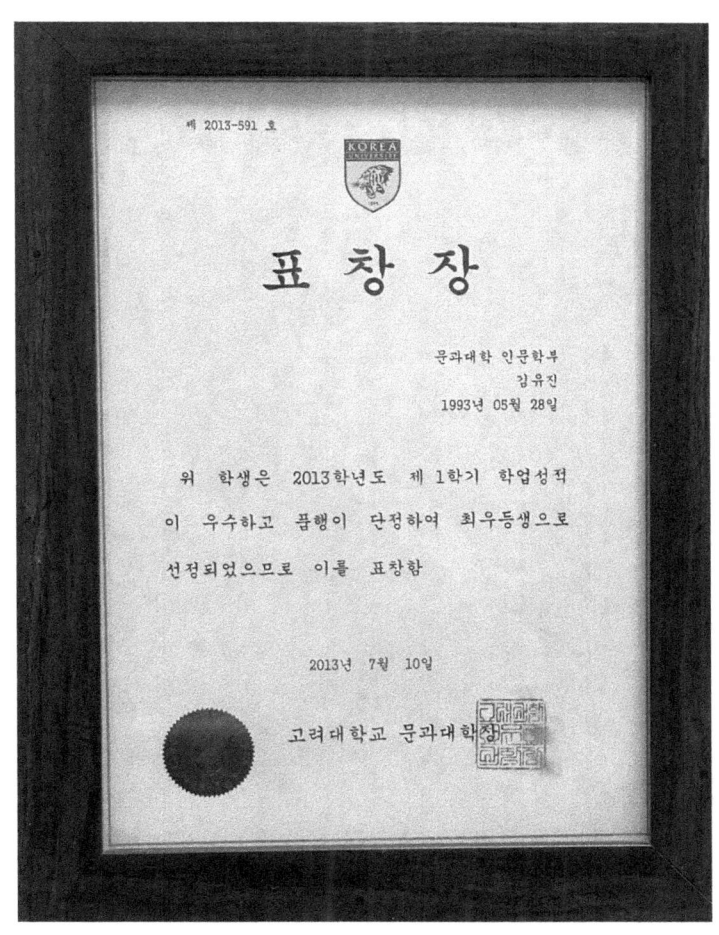

Academic award from Korea University

First time in America. The Library of Congress in Washington, DC

2

A BUMP ON THE ROAD

CHAPTER 4

SQUINTING

Broken—That Was What My Broken English Made Me Feel

Korean is a beautiful and sophisticated language that allows me to express the most complicated emotions and thoughts. When writing, I read the words out loud and smooth out the rough patches until the entire piece flows seamlessly. Like puzzle pieces perfectly put in place, it brings me joy to see my words—flawless and beautiful.

My love for the Korean language stretched to other languages, including English. When I was a child, I stood in front of the mirror in my room and practiced introducing myself in English. How it sounded, how it looked, and how it flowed—I loved everything about it. I studied English with love and curiosity.

Professor Roselyn was the professor of my first writing class at BU. Her course was notoriously convoluted even among native speakers, covering philosophical literature and the western classics. Even if the course seemed daunting, I signed up for the class because I liked having those philosophical conversations that would rarely happen outside of the classroom. Plus, the easier courses were already full, so this was the only class I could sign up for.

On the first day at school, I walked down an aisle with my headphones on. Still feeling the first-time nerves, I listened to music so the world could disappear into the background. The gold interior and high ceiling of the university didn't help ease my nervousness. It seemed like many other students felt the same way, listening to their own music so their worlds were still their own.

Walking into the rather small classroom, I was the only one who looked like me among twenty students sitting in the room—an Asian student fresh off the boat. The first part—Asian—was less important than the second part. Skin color did not matter to me. In my eyes, the contrast between American- versus foreign-born stood out more than the differences in our skin colors. Asian Americans were locals; they grew up here and spoke English fluently. At that time, I thought, America must be home to them. They must feel like they belong here, at least more than I do.

Breaking the silence, Professor Roselyn stepped into the classroom. She looked like someone who just jumped out of a movie, from some British street with a red payphone on a rainy day with her slight British accent, blond bob, and a long black coat that came down to her ankle—though I was sure she was American. Because of her soft voice, I hardly understood what she said. She was an add-on to a world that was already intimidating enough. My stuttering was at its worst around her.

The first reading was *The Stranger* by Albert Camus. The novel reflected Camus's belief that things happen with no apparent reasons or orders, and thus, life has no meaning. Karmas, miracles, serendipity, and dreams were made up by humans, who could not handle the discomfort of the uncertainty of life. Camus lived free from social and cultural constraints and died at the age of forty-four, quite inexplicably, from a sudden car accident.

I disagreed with him. I believed things happen for a reason, and we can shape our own world. I couldn't wait to write about my own views and how they may contrast Camus' beliefs. After finishing the first draft of my paper, I went through my editing ritual by reading it out loud and finding the rough patches to be cut out and smoothened. But I could not find them. Not because they were already perfect, but because I could not see them.

Is this good? I asked myself, expecting the answer to come back either in yes or no. But the answer was *I don't know.* There was no vision for the perfect sentence in my head. There was nothing to compare my rough sentences with.

Even though many Koreans learned English as children, we spoke Korean predominantly at home and at school. Plus, I learned English like mathematics, focusing on rules and sorting out the right answer from the wrong answers. With the little exposure to English and rigid way of learning, I could read but not really write; I could listen but not really speak.

I submitted the paper in the best shape possible, hoping my messages still shone through. When the professor returned the paper a few weeks later, I saw a C with red scrambles of words all over the papers.

In her unrecognizable scrambles of comments, I only saw one message: "No, this is not good."

I was one of those few who had beaten the odds. The things that happened to me, from getting into Korea University to being selected as a delegate for Korean American Student Conference, taught me dreams can come true. Losing what I was proud of and identified myself with, my past efforts, my talent, and my voice, I now started questioning whether these moments were just coincidences. As Camus believed, what if there were no miracles or magic, despite how much we wanted to believe so? What if this was the end of the story, and all my dreams stayed as dreams?

These questions remained unanswered, but I was busy rebuilding what would make me feel confident and proud. Visiting the writing center as frequently as I could, my grade in the writing course went from C to B. In the subsequent semesters, I got straight As and was on the dean's list, graduating magna cum laude one semester earlier than planned. The thing is fear was what pushed me to run as fast as I could. I made all these achievements while trembling inside as if I was missing my backbone. I did it because I had not yet learned how to live without pride.

* * *

Over time, I realized English was so tricky that even native speakers make quite a few mistakes. Knowing a lot of words did not matter that much in practice because Americans generally do not use big words both in written and verbal communications. Also, people who use English as a primary language spoke different English depending on where they were from—western countries like the US, UK, or Australia or Asian countries like Singapore or India. Some second-generation immigrants were sometimes confused about English because they use their parents' language at home more. Because of this diversity within the English language, making sense seemed to be more important than being grammatically correct—at least in day-to-day conversation.

However, it is normal to feel self-conscious about the language ability with or without having this knowledge. I also let my broken English eat away at my confidence. Sometimes, other people reinforced this insecurity by pointing out my pronunciation or making a non-verbal expression—"squinting."

A few months after I arrived in Boston, I met Professor Grace Lee. She was a Korean woman who studied mental health issues surrounding minority populations in a nonprofit research institute. I found out about her while exploring research assistant opportunities. How did she establish herself in America? What brought her to study mental health issues specifically for minority populations, and what did she find out about the issues? When I reached out to her, she was running multiple research projects and could use my help. I worked for Professor Grace Lee for one year.

She hustled, coming to the office at five in the morning, running a team of researchers and assistants, and giving talks on a radio show and in the news—all while raising three boys. As one of her research assistants, I said yes to all opportunities coming my way, from writing newsletters to transcribing a dozen interviews of minority women experiencing depression. And all these yeses led to more opportunities. I ended up speaking with a reporter who featured Professor Lee and me in a school magazine. Grace was my role model. She made it possible for me to imagine success in America.

But I had broken English. *Broken*—nothing should be called as such, but that was what my English made me feel. I tried to hide it by mimicking the American accent, but I stuttered even more. My broken English made me think something was wrong with me and my brain, making me wonder why I couldn't speak like a native person despite all the English vocabulary and grammar I knew. I wondered if it would ever be possible to speak in English like my mother tongue, and if it wouldn't, whether I would make it in America.

Sometimes, day-to-day interactions reinforced my language insecurity. One day, I went to see a professor who I felt quite close with. [8] He was approachable, funny, and helpful. During his office hours, we were going over homework. I told him, "I am comfortable with this question."

He said, "You are what?"

"Comfortable?" I answered.

Then he laughed and corrected my accent, "Kuhmf-tr-bl."[9]

And he repeated it until I got it right, laughing out loud. I repeated his pronunciation, watching him laugh and feeling confused and embarrassed. I got it only after five times. While I did feel close to him and didn't want to take offense, his laughs left a bitter taste in my mouth when I left his office.

I was not easily offended when people corrected how I spoke a word. Sometimes, people wanted to correct my pronunciation so I could communicate better. But I could not pronounce some words like a native speaker because my first language has a whole different set of alphabets and sounds. My ears did not differentiate some sounds, and my mouth wasn't used to producing those sounds. My accent or my speaking patterns were not something I could change with a snap of my fingers.

---

8   Though it is not the point which university this event happened at, this isn't necessarily from Boston University.

9   I know he was not making fun of me but am not sure what his laughs were for. I would like to think he was trying to diffuse the situation.

My broken English was not only about the language, but it was also about not knowing communication norms and political correctness. I used to work together with Professor Grace's assistants in an office. One of them was Sadia. When I first met her, her big eyes and brown skin had me interested in her ethnicity. I didn't know whether it'd be appropriate to ask this question. Should I ask where her parents came from? Or should I ask where she came from? I decided it would be better to be direct rather than going around the bush.

"What ethnicity are you?" I asked.

"Pakistani," she answered.

Wow, she's mastered the American accent, I thought and said, "You're very pretty."

Sadia laughed and said thank you.

Later that year, summer was approaching, so the room was full of excitement. Many of us looked forward to visiting our families. Half of the assistants were international students from China, Turkey, and Korea, and the other half were from somewhere in the US like San Francisco and Florida. We were chatty, just like normal college students on campus.

"Sadia, when do you go back to your country?" I asked.

The room became quiet.

"You meant, California?" Sadia answered, breaking the silence.

"California? I thought you were from Pakistan."

Then I saw a body language that I'd never seen before. It was squinting—like when people with bad vision narrow their eyes. It was saying, *I can't believe you just said that*. I heard it, though it was not spoken. I said to her, "Sorry, I misunderstood," to which Sadia said, "It's okay" with an awkward smile. I tried to make up for it by changing the topic, but I only had one thought: *I think I made a mistake.*

The squinting was subtle but powerful. It was a way to express that what I said or did was not right. The message was unspoken, but it was there. Because it was not obvious, it was scarier. It added a dose of unknowns and uncertainty, making me overthink my words and behaviors, and even more so as I was in a country that was thousands of miles away from home. Often, no words were said when people squinted. They just did it and moved on, leaving me to feel ashamed and anxious.

The squinting was everywhere. It was in the classroom when I was struggling to ask questions to the professor. It was at the round table where I did group work with other students, trying to get my point across. It was in a casual conversation with my advisors, strangers, or anyone I met for the first time.

Later, I learned people can squint for reasons that aren't punitive. They were simply trying to understand what was being said, or they were trying to focus. I learned to ditch the guessing game and pretended it did not exist unless it was obvious. But the squinting was there, telling me to watch my thoughts and my words.

The squinting followed me everywhere, now in my head, filtering my thoughts and words, to Dunkin Donuts, to friendly parties, and to interviews. The girl who told herself, *You got this*, the girl who chased her ambition now took a deep breath first before ordering a cup of coffee. Conversations, good or bad, haunted me, reeling and repeating in my head, telling me, *That was stupid*. This state of mind, nagging and confusing, sucked energy out of me, and so did the people in my head telling me, *You fucked up*.

* * *

Over time, I became more fluent in both speaking and writing. I got used to how native speakers used the language, and I was able to tell whether my sentences made sense. I could think and dream in English, and people would be surprised to know I had only lived here for a few years after hearing me speak. I continued feeling unsure about my words, but at the time, I couldn't pinpoint the source of insecurity.

I went to graduate school at Tufts University in 2018, a year after I graduated from BU. Many of my cohorts at the graduate program were international students who looked like me. They were from Korea or China, and some were from India. Jin was one of the Chinese students in my graduate program. She stood out to me because of the way she seamlessly and adequately interacted with professors, even if she struggled to finish her sentences. When she couldn't think of words, she didn't hide it and said, "I forgot what that was called!" The language barriers didn't seem to bother her, unlike me who was acutely aware of them even though my English was more fluent than hers.

I got to know her better as we were in the same group for a project. When having conversations with her, I noticed my patience. I let her take her time and did not rush her to get her points across. Every mistake and pause she made was understandable because she had lived in the States for less than a year. She also spoke as if the language barriers did not exist, and that melted down the walls between us. Because I was comfortable with her unassuming way of communication, my English was a lot fluent around her as well.

She reminded me that anybody who comes to a new country would have a lot to learn when it comes to language, culture, and social norms. Then why was I demanding that I speak like a native and write like I would in my mother tongue? Why couldn't I show the same level of compassion toward myself as I would show to Jin?

Jin taught me that the source of my insecurity was the lack of self-compassion toward myself. English is not my first language, and it is okay to feel uncomfortable with it. I used to force myself to be more fluent and sound more American. I beat myself up for not being able to do so. Now, I focused on getting my messages across and took my time doing so. Ironically, this gave me peace of mind and led to more fluency and better communication with other people. Of course, I continued to work on my English by reading books and watching videos, which helped me feel more confident.

When I treated myself the way I treated Jin, my English no longer made me feel broken.

I showed myself strong compassion in other situations as well. If someone just arrived in Korea, she may not know it is only respectful to let the older person pour your drink while you're holding the glass. In America, that's what servers do. Newcomers shouldn't be expected to know every social rule. Since I respect other cultures and am open to learning, that's mainly what matters.

I still made mistakes, and the squinting was still there whether in reality or in my head. But it did not affect me as it used to. I could care less about the squinting because you, whoever is doing the squinting, would have done worse if you were me.

CHAPTER 5

STOPOVERS

Everywhere Is Somewhere I Stop By

After a few years of living in America, I learned a difference between the feeling of *different* and *out of place*. In high school, I felt different from other students as one of the few girls rebelling against regulations. In my hometown, I felt different from others as one of the few who made it to SKY and to America. Still, I felt I was a part of these communities and didn't doubt whether I belonged or not. Deep down, I knew we had shared experiences that allowed us to connect if we wanted to.

In America, I felt different and out of place. On top of feeling different, I did not quite belong to where I was, whether I was with other international students, other Koreans, or my neighbors. Wherever I went, I felt like an add-on to a group that otherwise has a complete and harmonious identity. We shared very few experiences, and the gaps between us seemed insurmountable.

My sense of otherness started developing when I lived in Lowell, my first home in America. Lowell is about an hour away from Boston by car and is a diverse neighborhood with half of the residents being minorities, mainly Cambodians. The downtown area had Massachusetts's signature brick buildings and was vibrant with local stores, restaurants, and bars. It also suffered from drug problems and homelessness. Strangely enough, I never saw a single Korean in Lowell even though Lowell had a large university.

My friend Eli and I lived together with a couple, Dan and Ava. Dan was one of the friendliest guys I knew. I never saw him speak badly about other people or get angry at someone. His nonchalant personality, generosity, and loyalty attracted many friends and family members to him. Ava was an independent woman with ambitions who loved candles and nature. She taught me how important it is for women to be self-sufficient and not to rely on a partner for financial support. And both of them loved smoking weed. Though I've always thought marijuana is a personal preference, I wasn't used to it; you can go to jail in Korea for that.

Dan and Eva called me Christine. Christine was the American name I gave to myself at Korea University. I picked Christine because I was a big fan of the actress Kristen Stewart. (I apparently didn't know how to spell her name.) I was used to picking an American name in my English classes since elementary school, so it felt like a nice thing to do for native-English speakers. As Christine, however, I had one less layer of Korean identity and didn't feel fully myself.[10]

The house was far from my school. I took the commuter rail to go to school, which took at least two hours and drained me by the end of the day. In a snowstorm, I would set my

---

10   I stopped using my American name by the time I graduated from Boston University. I felt like I wasn't fully myself when someone called me with a western name, since that was not where I came from.

alarm for five and check my phone with my eyes half open, hoping school got canceled. But it didn't happen as much as I hoped it would because my school did not close unless Harvard did. If school stayed open, Eli would drive me in a blizzard to the station, trying to see through the snow and maneuver the Prius on the slippery roads.

In Lowell, I was constantly exposed to what I wasn't used to—drugs, debilitating commutes, and never-ending snow, all while using a western name and not having a single Korean person around me. The unfamiliarity made Lowell feel like a stopover—somewhere I stay only temporarily and would soon leave for somewhere else. That place, I hoped, offered things that made me feel like I belong.

The thing is, Boston didn't give me that sense of belongingness I was missing. Because I lived so far from the campus, I wasn't fully integrated into the community. I was a guest to this beautiful campus, which offered a different experience than the neighborhood I lived in. The school occasionally provided food and dessert to research assistants and professors on tables covered with red velvet tablecloths by the Charles River. Professors worked as economic counselors to the White House and spoke on national news. Alumni achieved their dreams in politics, sports, businesses, and academia. In Boston, I saw a glimpse of hope and security but wasn't sure if that was meant for me.

I also didn't quite fit in the profile of East Asian international students commonly seen in Boston, like one of my best friends Chelsea.[11] I met Chelsea in an international trade class. She was an adorable, petite woman who brought a Hermès

---

11 We were able to become best friends because I was never jealous of what she had. To me, her financial status was one aspect of her life.

bag to school. I couldn't even estimate how many designer items she owned because they changed by season and trend. She regularly invited me to her apartment in Boston that overlooked the entire downtown and the Charles River. She had an impressive collection of shoes and bags: almost all colors of the newest Gucci loafers and quite a few Louboutin shoes. On my birthday, she handed me a Hermès scarf that was exclusive to their VIP members. Later, I learned her father owned a financial company in China. Her parents already had a job for her, though she didn't seem interested.

Her financial cushion seemed to afford her a lifestyle that seemed pressure-free. While I loaded my semesters with twenty-one credits to graduate early and worked as a research assistant for Professor Grace, she took exactly what was required and did not worry about building her resume. She seemed to have options, like her collection of designers, which could save her from inconveniences whenever she wanted to. That to me was the taste of security, the taste of a breathing room, the mental and physical space that saves yourself some tiny bit of inconvenience, effort, and decency. This was what I saw in many East Asian international students at BU, and I felt I was the only one worried about money.

I didn't feel like I entirely belonged in Boston—there was something buoyant and extravagant about it that made me feel out of place. Like Lowell, Boston was also a stopover for me even though I wasn't quite sure where I was heading to.

* * *

We moved to Eli's parents' house in Lynn a year after to get closer to our schools. Lynn was Eli's hometown and an urban neighborhood with the old reputation of "the city of sin." Like

Eli had said, Lynn had struggled with gang violence and poverty in some parts. I heard noises at night, which I couldn't tell if they were gunshots or fireworks. Many of people I met in Lynn were hardworking people who valued education and friendship, but some people on the street seemed like they were on drugs.

Not seeing Korean people around me made me feel I wasn't fitting into my neighborhood. I wondered if I would feel a sense of belongingness if I met more Korean people, so I looked for a Korean restaurant near to the campus in Arlington and brought Eli there. It was a restaurant that sold *sundubu jjigae* or tofu soup. I sat down with her and read through the menu. While we were choosing our foods, a Korean lady brought out some Korean side dishes—*kimchi*, scallion pancakes, salted shrimps, and stir-fried fishcake.

I ordered my *sundubu jjigae* in Korean and looked around. I saw many Korean students and families. That little place brought me back to Korea, and I felt like I belonged. I never realized how much impact my Korean identity had on me.

Then I remembered how my grandmother, a lifelong Christian, would ask me whether I found a church in America. She said the church would make me feel connected socially and spiritually. In the beginning, I brushed off her words with, "Will do," but I started thinking I should give it a try. Maybe I could find the belongingness I felt missing for over a year.

I knew quite a few Korean churches were in Massachusetts, even though they were far from where I lived. I reached out to a youth pastor in a Korean church in Boston. Ji-Soo was a BU student studying Christianity. I asked her about how to get started, and with warmth and kindness, she invited me to the church.

On a cold Sunday morning, I got onto the T, the metro. The church was in Brookline, a quieter and cleaner neighborhood in Boston. It was still early, so I grabbed a breakfast panini and an Americano at a café to keep myself warm.

What a beautiful city this is, I thought, sitting at a table facing outside.

The sky was clear, shining a light on everyone and everything on the streets. The coffee warmed up my entire body, convincing me that everything would go well. In a country that was a couple of thousand miles from Korea, I was about to reconnect with my roots I hadn't gotten in touch with in the past two years—my Korean identity and Christianity.

The church service was mostly in Korean with English subtitles. It was enjoyable even though I wasn't used to being around so many Koreans. I felt the sense of connection arising inside of me; this was a community, where people celebrate life, sympathize with pain, and exchange blessings with each other. These could be my people who would help me stay grounded.

After the service, Ji-Soo invited me over coffee to get to know one another better, where I got to meet the pastor as well. The pastor started asking where I lived and where I studied. I said I lived in Lowell, to which he said, "Wow, you traveled all the way here?" I asked him where people at the church usually lived. He said they usually lived in Brookline or Cambridge. Then he asked why I hadn't visited any Korean churches yet, to which I said the thought just didn't come across to my mind.

Insecurity can make you an overthinker. When you are insecure about how you dress, for example, you become so conscious that someone's comments about your clothes can make you overthink the intention behind them—even if the intention was positive. Because I was insecure about how different I was for the past two years, these innocent comments triggered me to think, *Am I that different from you?*

Then my mind started making assumptions. These Koreans lived in similar neighborhoods, while I was one of the few who lived outside of Boston. Our roots were not likely the same, either. They were probably Koreans who already made it in America, already went to some of the best universities in the world, and already worked at top-notch organizations. I assumed they were from money and well-connected Gangnam families. They all likely graduated from the same high school, the ones Mr. Kim said dominated SKY.

Granted, these assumptions didn't come out of nowhere. In Boston, I met several Korean students who were upper-class Koreans from some of the most affluent areas in Seoul. They went to the same upper-class high school, and one of their parents was a pioneering ophthalmologist. They already had their own circles of Korean friends. I didn't fully grasp why they had such homogeneous friend groups, though I now understand it may be their way to cope with their own sense of otherness. Because of these differences, I felt we would never be able to connect at a deeper level. I sometimes felt I was looked down on for my limited English and connections, but these thoughts are always hard to prove.

However, there is a caveat in making assumptions about new people based on experience: I pulled myself away from building meaningful connections without giving them a chance. Maybe I would have gotten along with some people at the church, regardless of their backgrounds. Maybe I might have met someone who came from my hometown; then we'd have bonded so well. If anyone judged me based on my circumstances, they were in the wrong, not me.

I stopped going to the church in the following week, and the church became another stopover. Ji-Soo followed up with me quite a few times, asking why I hadn't shown up to the church. She wasn't pushy. I believe she saw how isolated I was with minimal social circles and experiences in the States. Like my grandmother, she seemed to believe I could feel at home and connected with others at her church. And she wasn't the only one who tried to help. Another Korean woman I met at school wanted to get me to do some community activities, but I made excuses.

The sense of otherness I felt at the church made me think searching for belongingness can be a futile effort. Even though I was with other people who shared cultural backgrounds, I could always make myself feel out of place by creating assumptions and finding differences. As someone who moved into this diverse country in her early twenties, it may not make sense to find that connection I felt in Korea.

Instead of searching for a place to put down my roots, then, I'd be better off by seeing myself as a *traveler*.

This was how I saw myself as an exchange student in Vancouver in 2015, right before transferring to BU. I knew I would stay there only for four months and focused on relishing this opportunity to experience a new place. I occasionally traveled downtown with some other exchange students or traveled solo to Vancouver Island. I loved exploring the campus, which was quite like a national park, checking out the buildings, lakes, and museums before stopping for a delicious brunch. After the exploration was over, I came back to my dormitory and made myself feel at home by connecting with the people and food I loved and was familiar with.

In Vancouver, I didn't ask myself whether I belonged or not.

The question didn't matter; I was already enriched with new experiences.

Now two years later since I studied in Vancouver, I came full circle and saw myself as a traveler again. As a traveler, I valued both newness and familiarity. I was okay with being the only Korean person in the neighborhood. That was a signal that there were many people and things I could get to know of. At the same time, I filled my life with the things I loved and was familiar with—by cooking Korean food and spending time with my family back home. This way, I had the best of both worlds; I was growing and content.

I realized many people around me were also travelers—whether at school or in my neighborhood. They may or may not have had a permanent home in America, but they were also newcomers. I felt deeply connected with these other travelers—who braved the uncertainty and called multiple places home. I started seeing myself living somewhere with lots of travelers; maybe, after all the stopovers, that was where I was heading.

CHAPTER 6

SECRET BOX

When Diversity Expands or Shrinks Us

———

Growing up in Korea, I wasn't used to living with differences. Korea is ethnically and culturally homogeneous with over 90 percent of the population being Korean. I listened to K-pop music, watched K-dramas, and ate Korean food. I was only exposed to a handful of other cultures, including American, Japanese, and British.

Because I wasn't exposed to diverse cultures, things seemed odd or even *crazy* if they were different than what I was used to. At Korea University, I learned that people in some countries like Argentina and India eat dinner around nine. Because I had been eating my dinner at six o'clock for over twenty years, I thought it was unusual that people could eat so late.

When I first came to Massachusetts in 2016, I was amazed by many different types of food available—Mexican, Jamaican, Indian, Chinese, and European. My friend Eli loved Mexican food so much she brought me to a Mexican restaurant at least once a week. We went to the most authentic ones in Massachusetts where the servers spoke Spanish to me and to the most franchised ones like Taco Bell. I loved tacos; I loved how light yet filling they were and how they perfectly balanced out the number of carbs, protein, and vegetables.

However, I had one problem with tacos: cilantro. The innocuous herb made the entire dish taste like... soap. I was with Eli when I first tried cilantro, and I almost spit it out. Eli saw my face and asked me whether my food was okay.

"Something... tastes weird," I said while trying hard not to sound rude.

Eli laughed and said, "I think you tried cilantro."

"Cilantro! What the heck is that?" I said with a frown on my face.

She pointed out the little herb in my taco. With a cautious look on my face, I picked some of them and tasted them— and yes, that was the culprit! I immediately took out all the cilantro from my taco, but my food was already flavored with cilantro. I had to give the rest of my tacos to Eli and went home with an empty stomach.

After I discovered my abhorrence toward cilantro, I made a point of taking out cilantro every time I ordered South Asian or Hispanic dishes. When I forgot about doing it, I acted as if I had made the biggest mistake of my life; how dare I ruin my dish again? Often, I took out the cilantro immediately, minimized the damage, and ate the food because I didn't want to starve.

A year after during winter, my sister Yenny visited me from Korea. We traveled together to New York City, and we wanted to get a bowl of pho to fight off the weather. We ordered our food at a popular Vietnamese restaurant in the city located near Chinatown. When the bowls came out, I realized I forgot to take out the cilantro. Again! Feeling terrible about ruining my dish, I took a sip of the juicy-looking pho that would have otherwise been perfect.

Then I came to a strange realization: I didn't want my soup in any other way. Actually, I wanted more cilantro. The cilantro added a refreshing flavor to my entire soup that could otherwise be dull and meaty. At that moment, I not only learned the taste but also loved the taste. I was officially converted from a cilantro hater to a cilantro lover, and this could never be undone.

Cilantro taught me a simple life lesson: I can change. Then the world became full of possibilities: This meant I could enjoy, love, and feel happy about so many things in the world even if I haven't discovered them yet.

Because of these "cilantro" moments, I became curious and open-minded toward other people's stories. I wanted to see whether I could enjoy, love, and feel happy about more things. I was especially interested in people's stories from countries I only saw in the textbook—Argentina, Guatemala, and Costa Rica. Some people came to the States because their country was no longer safe to stay, and others wanted freedom and opportunities America could offer. Their stories taught me there were truly different ways of life, and none of them were right or wrong.

More "cilantro" moments in my life occurred—when what I wasn't familiar with or didn't like became one of my favorite things. They were the Spanish language, *Pahok* (Cambodian fish paste), and blonde balayage. Every time I unlocked one more cilantro moment, I felt I expanded and grew as a person; and this had made my life feel like a secret box of gifts—full of unexpected but delightful surprises.

* * *

Ironically, diversity also shrank me. Since I was around a mixed group of people, my Korean background sometimes outweighed the rest of my personality or experience. People asked me many times where I was from, and at friends' gatherings, I was introduced as Korean.

I noticed a set of cultural expectations that I was supposed to be a certain way if I was "a real Korean." All of a sudden, I was asked about the hottest Korean restaurants, K-dramas, and Korean churches. When I said I didn't know about those, I would get a surprised look with "How so?" I did not know how to answer that question, so I mumbled some reasons I think why I wasn't "Korean enough." I lived far from Boston, which afforded me little time exploring Korean restaurants. At the time, I also grew out of watching dramas or movies and instead enjoyed YouTube videos.

But the Korean identity was in my DNA; I lived there for over twenty years. I can't live without *kimchi* and always need a large jar of it in my fridge. I know a thing or two about maintaining healthy skin. I value punctuality and efficiency; this is tied to the *"pali-pali"* culture that literally means "hurry, hurry" and reflects Koreans' tendency for doing things quickly. (If opening my internet browser takes longer than two seconds, there's something wrong with the Wi-Fi!) Whenever I leaned heavily into my Korean culture or behaviors, I was called "too Korean."

It worked out for me that the stereotypes attached to my Korean identity were generally positive. In many people's eyes, Koreans were harmless with their motto being "work hard and play hard." From BTS to *Squid Game*, our culture was great for small talk. I got more compliments on my skin and makeup in America than I did in Korea. My passport allowed me to travel almost anywhere in the world without scrutiny. (Oh, except our neighboring country, North Korea.)

I remembered walking into a postal office to ship an item, and the cashier kept repeating my name: "Yujin, Yujin... You must be Korean."

I gave him a friendly smile and said, "Yes, I am."

With a big smile on his face, he said, "I love Korean people! I used to live close to a Korean couple. Such nice people. Such beautiful people."

"Oh, great! I'm glad you had a great experience with Korean people," I said.

He handed me the receipt, bowing and saying thank you in Korean: *"Kam-sa-hap-ni-da."*

Leaving the post office, I thought about how privileged I was that people were so friendly just because of my culture. It was common that someone I first met would tell me, "You're Korean? Great! I always wanted to make Korean friends. We should hang out sometime." I even met people who said they would only date Korean guys. They would even marry one if the guy looked like their favorite K-pop star. (That's okay; a girl can dream!)

Whenever my nationality gathered invitations like this, I couldn't help but ask myself whether they wanted to hang out with me because they liked me or because I was Korean.

Of course, I loved that people were interested in my culture. I loved clearing up the questions, stereotypes, and misconceptions that people have about my country.

Then what's the issue?

Like my career, the neighborhood I live in, and where I came from, my Korean identity is a part of who I am. Thus, I am comfortable when it is treated as such. When my culture started defining or overriding who I am, I felt like other people put me in a box. Both positive and negative, the cultural expectation triggered me to compare who I was to who I was supposed to be.

* * *

Unfortunately, my Asian identity wasn't always advantageous. When I didn't say anything because I had nothing to say, some people told me not to be shy. When I didn't complain because I had nothing to complain about, I was worried whether I was reinforcing the stereotype that Asians usually put their heads down, work hard, and don't complain. A couple of times, I experienced blunt racism especially when I was with other Asian women—like when some dudes yelled Chinese words at me while driving past us. Seeing us startled, they waved and laughed, disappearing into the road ahead.

Whenever this happened, I brushed it off. They were the stupid ones, not me.

But that changed recently in 2021 when the severity of racism toward Asian people came to the surface.

By this time, I had moved to Washington, DC. It was nine in the evening in the US and ten in the morning in South Korea. My family and I were on FaceTime while they were having a late breakfast. In the middle of chatting and laughing, my dad cleared his throat and asked me a question.

"So, do they not like Asians over there?"

My dad tended not to show his worries about me. He trusted I knew what I was doing and gave me guidance only when I asked for it. But this time, he brought up his concerns.

The look on my father's face caught me off guard because I could tell he tried to pretend that he wasn't worried.

I realized there was no good way to answer him. I didn't want to hide anything but didn't want him to worry.

"Well, I heard a lot about things going on in San Francisco and New York City…"

I paused, carefully selecting my words.

"But I think things are better in DC."

He nodded. I didn't know if my answer made him feel better anyway. I didn't know how I was feeling either because I hadn't processed this myself. We didn't talk about this topic afterward, but I couldn't forget the look on my dad's face.

The next day, I saw on the news that a man pushed an eighty-four-year-old Asian man in San Francisco. He died from this incident outside of his house. As the media started paying more attention to the crimes targeting people of Asian descent, people started asking me how I was doing. I also started asking people how they were doing.

I always carried pepper spray with me because I never felt safe in America. But I never needed it because violence never breathed so close to me before. When my family and friends started worrying about my safety, I understood I could be a target. One day, I went to the nearby park and found a place that was far away from other people. I tested my pepper spray on the ground and walked away from it, watching the powders subside, praying I never had to use it.

Coming home from the park, I started walking as far away from other people as I could get. If they got a bit closer to me, I would get my spray ready. My fear grew so rapidly that everyone seemed like a threat.

I thought I was doing a pretty good job at navigating my ethnic identity. I made conscious efforts not to put myself in any box so I did not get caught up in others' expectations of me. However, I sometimes caught myself feeding the stereotypes saying things like, "Because I'm Asian!" It was convenient; I was not responsible for my traits that many other Asians happened to share. I did not need to explain why I cared so much about my grades and career.

Then I started seeing how unhealthy it could be. First of all, saying yes to the stereotyping gave others permission to stereotype me. Even beyond this, I was giving myself permission to put others in a box. By doing this, I would miss my opportunity to get to know someone as who they are, and even worse, I would actively stop individualism from prospering—the very thing I came to America for.

But I never realized my ethnicity could physically hurt me. This form of racism felt foreign to me.

What should I do? How do I keep myself safe?

I could guard up, trying to look for the signs that the person could be harmful.

Or I could give the benefit of doubt that the person was harmless until it becomes obvious they were not.

And I stood somewhere between these two options, slightly leaning toward the second one. And of course, my judgment might be wrong. Of course, I would be reasonably cautious, and sometimes I had to make a judgment based on how the person carried themselves. But in normal circumstances, I would not want to mistake someone as harmful when they were harmless.

At least this way, I came from the place of trust, rather than the place of fear.

After coming back home from the park, I watched the news on my tablet reporting the incident in San Francisco. Then it grabbed my attention that the media was only talking about Asian Americans or AAPI (Asian Americans and Pacific Islanders) but not about how these racist behaviors affect non-Americans including international students and expatriates. I went ahead and researched Asian hate crimes, and few places were inclusive of non-American Asian populations.

The surge of hate crimes added insecurity and fear to the lives of all Asian people, not just those born in America. In fact, one of the main motives for this crime was xenophobia, thinking "foreigners" had brought insecurity to their life, in terms of job security, education opportunities, and health crisis. That was a double punch to our guts because the hate crimes scared us too, and now we were being excluded from the conversation.

I wouldn't know whether the exclusion was deliberate. All I knew was this made the wall between foreign- and American-born Asian populations feel more palpable when that was the last thing we needed.

I closed my tablet to give myself a break. I took a deep breath thinking about the irony of diversity. Diversity could be a secret box of gifts presenting us with serendipity to grow and expand, but it could also shrink us into a smaller box with stronger labels. Diversity was the richness of life for some people and was the source of division to others.

In the end, I did not have control over what other people would do with it. I just understood I could play my part by celebrating the richness of our cultures while still respecting the different walks of life each of us has created.

CHAPTER 7

BABY ADULT

Learning to Live on My Own Terms

———

In America, I felt like a baby adult. I was a twenty-four-year-old adult, but I didn't know how things worked around me. I didn't know where to go to get the things I needed. I didn't know how to drive and how my health insurance worked. I didn't know how to ask for help. Even though Eli helped me to figure out a lot of things, that reliance only made me feel more incompetent.

Being a baby adult not only disempowered me but also led to some detrimental mistakes, including one I made on May 28, 2017, my twenty-fourth birthday.

This was my second time celebrating my birthday in America. The only friend who knew about my birthday was Eli, but she was away for her research conference in Ohio. I read through the birthday wishes from my family and friends back in Korea. All of these used to make me happy—birthdays and friendship—but they became something to be figured out. I had to try to make friends, make plans, and even celebrate my birthday. In Korea, it was our family tradition to celebrate each other's birthday, but here, I had nobody who did that for me.

I was laying down on my bed, and my phone started ringing. It was Ava, one of my previous roommates. Eli must have told Dan and Ava it was my birthday and I probably didn't have any plans. I picked up the phone, and they convinced me to come out, saying no one is supposed to spend their birthday alone.

"Sorry, I don't feel good," I said to Ava. Even though I was grateful for their invitation, I was ashamed. I felt like a loner who didn't have any close friends. If I already felt so down, I would end up not enjoying myself in their company. Ava kept trying to get me out, but I shut her down.

I tucked my phone under the pillow and lay down on the bed while hearing a million voices fighting in my head.

I should have gone out.
This is why no one remembers my birthday.
It's better to stay in if I can't enjoy myself.
I can't believe Eli's away. She ruined it.
A birthday is just a birthday. It is what it is!

These voices became louder and louder, pushing me in different directions. I spent at least an hour lying on my bed and not knowing what to do with my thoughts. Then I started feeling bad for myself. I was so sorry that I was me. I felt like I wouldn't need to go through all these struggles if I had stayed in Korea. Then I wouldn't have left behind so many things that made me happy—my family, our little celebrations, my squad, and my hometown. What the hell was wrong with me?

I cried for the first time after coming to America. Everything I experienced—my language insecurity, the sense of otherness, and incompetence—all came together and struck me at once. I cried laying on my bed and pulled the blanket all the way to my head, even though no one could hear me from my basement room. After hours' worth of tears, I fell asleep.

When I woke up, I had clarity like a sunbeam shining through the clouds. I thought there must be a way to end all these conflicting thoughts, worries, and voices that had held me back from living my life to its fullest.

I wanted to talk to someone who could give me insight into what I was going through in this new world. Someone who could keep things to themselves. Someone who could listen to me with no strings attached.

I got up from my bed and sat down at my desk. I found out I could send an anonymous text to the campus police anytime in a day. I thought they could give me the guidance for who I could talk to—after all, they were the campus police looking after the safety and well-being of students.

I sent them an anonymous text saying I was having anxiety and conflicting thoughts. Immediately after, they responded to me asking whether I'd like to meet them and explain the situation in person. I agreed to meet them on campus the next day.

The day after, I stood in front of the main building, and the campus police officer pulled over. When he asked me how he could help, I cried again even though I thought there was nothing left in my chest. But this time, I was relieved and connected knowing someone was helping me (even though a crying female student and the police didn't seem to relieve anyone else).

The officer told me he could bring me to a hospital where I could talk to a therapist or psychiatrist.

"Would you like to see them?" he asked.

I nodded, not knowing what I was getting myself into.

Ten minutes later, an ambulance arrived. I started feeling that things were evolving too quickly, and I might lose control over the situation. Still unsure, I went into the ambulance and sat on the white bed, watching the emergency technician checking my heart rates and blood pressure.

I arrived in an emergency room. I wasn't sure whether I was supposed to be here, but I was so exhausted from crying. When I was laying down on my bed, a nurse came in and checked on me: "Do you have an insurance card?"

An insurance card? I didn't know I was supposed to bring it with me all the time. That would be old-fashioned; wouldn't they have a database to look up my information? I remembered how in Korea the nurse could easily find information from the database.

"No, I don't," I answered.

She looked at me with a concerned look on her face.

"Do you have insurance?"

I knew I had one because I had to argue with a school administrator not to have insurance. It was $3,500 per year on top of my exorbitant tuition fees. I told the nurse I should have insurance through my school, and somehow, she found my information and registered me in the system.

As she left, she told me with a low and warm voice, "It's just a small bump in the road."

I had never heard of this expression, but I liked it. Just a small bump in the road. I might have driven off the bump too fast, but that would pass. I would be on the road again because it was just a small bump in the road.

The bed felt strangely comfortable, and I fell in and out of sleep. The nurse came in again and told me a psychiatrist would come and check on me in an hour. She also gave me food until I met the psychiatrist. Then as softly as possible, she whispered, "*Don't tell him everything.*"

What? I was here to tell everything to someone so I could figure out what was wrong with me.

"What do you mean?" I asked, now wide awake.

"You heard me," she said and walked away.

After a couple of hours, the psychiatrist opened the white blinds around my bed and stood next to the bedside. He wore round black glasses and looked as tired as I was.

Finally, I can pick his brain, I thought.

I explained to him that I had running thoughts that held me back. They were often negative ones. They drained me of energy. They stopped me from connecting with people and meeting new ones. But I know all of them were in my head, and I wanted to stop living in my head. I explained that I actually spent a whole day on my bed the day before, and it was my birthday.

He wrote down my answers on his clipboard. After I finished explaining, he checked my eyes. He asked if I was on any medication and if I was diagnosed with any mental illness. I said no.

"Have you ever had suicidal thoughts?" he asked.

I never hurt myself or planned for it, but *yes*, I thought about what would happen if I disappeared. Well, that would not be a great idea because I loved my family and myself. But I was exhausted from running as fast as I could to rebuild my past, being isolated from people and my communities, and dealing with the future uncertainty. I would never kill myself, but *yes*, I thought about it. Doesn't everyone do at least once in their life?

He nodded and wrote down what I said. Then he left, wishing me well.

A couple of people, including the nurse, came in and moved my bed to somewhere else. I asked the nurse, "Wait, where am I going?"

She looked at me and said, "You are staying somewhere safe just for a couple of days."

It was as if she woke me up from a nightmare, but reality was as bad as my nightmare.

This ain't it, I thought.

The nurse left, wishing me well.

* * *

The ambulance felt small and made me claustrophobic. They didn't restrain me, but I felt trapped. Things were evolving so quickly I didn't know where it went wrong. Regardless, I had to know where I was going. No beating around the bush, no sugarcoating.

"Where am I going?" I asked the man checking my blood pressure.

Sensing how irritated I was, he explained it was not a scary place. I could wear my personal clothes and see my family and friends.

"No, where am I really going?"

He said I was going somewhere called a behavioral center.

My mind went blank as if someone hit my head with something really hard and heavy. It terrified me knowing I was going to be, basically, sectioned. It was completely unwarranted; they didn't ask me how I felt about this. They didn't ask for my consent. I just needed someone to talk to, but this was what I got.

I arrived at the center an hour later. A woman came out and took my bag, shoes, and phone—basically everything except my clothes. She introduced her name as Sarah.

After I turned over my stuff, she walked me into the unit. I told her I came here without a proper assessment and demanded speaking with a doctor immediately. Sarah said she was not the right person to talk to about that. *The right person*. Right, one of the reasons why I was here was because I did not talk to the right person.

"Then, who is *the right person* to talk to?" I asked.

"The on-call doctor will be here shortly," she said.

Only one thing mattered at that moment: going home. At least I had my freedom there. At least I could have my own world, whether it made me happy or not. I stopped walking with her and refused to settle in my unit. I told her I would be waiting for the doctor in the visiting area.

After three hours, the doctor came in. He looked as tired as the psychiatrist did. His name was David, and he patiently listened to me explaining why I wasn't supposed to be here. I told him I even worked for a research team studying depression and suicidality. He sighed and said, "Then why did you say you had suicidal thoughts?"

"Don't people do that sometimes when they are sad? That doesn't mean they would do it. I was just describing how sad I felt!" I answered, frustrated.

"In America, people take that stuff really seriously," he answered.

"Then what do I do now?" I asked him, realizing how naive I was.

David said the most he could do was to discharge me as early as possible. People must stay at least three days at the center excluding holidays and weekends. I was admitted on Friday, so the earliest release would be on the following Wednesday. That was five days I would have to spend here.

After thanking David for his time, I walked inside the center past the visiting area with the essentials they gave me. There was a TV and a common area with a pile of drawing books and coloring pencils. Five or six people hung out in the common area, all wearing normal clothes and laughing as if they were in a coffee shop. I almost forgot where I was until I saw cuts on someone's arm and a girl who was as thin as paper.

Two of the patients were international students like me. They also came from East Asian countries: Japan and Korea. The Japanese girl told her counselor her uncle stressed her out so much she wanted to kill her uncle. The Korean guy told his therapist that he thought about committing suicide because of academic stress. They said they didn't know if their words would be taken so seriously. They were, like me, baby adults.

I shared a unit with a woman. I introduced myself briefly and laid down on my bed, thinking about how all this happened. This series of events—spending my birthday on the bed, having a breakdown, and coming here—felt like a black hole that sucked me in. It felt as if I was already walking toward this black hole for a long time, and my birthday was when I got close enough to give it power.

I tried to trace back when I started walking toward this black hole. Was it when I first came to Boston, realizing I had nothing to show? Was it when I started avoiding meeting new people and building my own shell? I was such a positive and optimistic person, but now I couldn't even recognize my past self. For the past two years, every day felt like a struggle.

Maybe, I was supposed to be here for a few days.

* * *

The next day, I asked Sarah to call Eli. Because I didn't remember her number, I asked Sarah to check my phone. When I got my phone back, I quickly emailed professors that I was hospitalized and would be released the upcoming Wednesday. I also texted my family that my phone was being fixed, and I would get it back by Wednesday. Then I wrote down Eli's numbers on a piece of paper, returned the phone, and headed to the phone area.

I called Eli and explained what happened and where I was. Eli had just come back from Ohio that morning. She didn't say anything for a moment, then asked me whether I was okay. She said she would visit me that afternoon.

At 4 p.m. when visiting hours started, Eli stepped into the visiting area. She teared up as soon as she saw me. I reassured her that I felt fine and sat with her at a table. We didn't bring up again how I ended up there. I asked her how her trip was, and she asked me whether I needed anything here. I made a joke, saying whatever it is, she couldn't bring anything with some sorts of strings or sharp ends because the center would take them away.

She also laughed at my joke and seemed more relaxed than when I first saw her. Then she said, "We'll figure it out, Yujin. We'll find a way." She reminded me how three years ago, I didn't know how I would come to America, but I eventually figured a way out of Korea. Everything in America, as much as it seemed so complicated, was all made by humans and I could figure them out. Whatever difficulties I was going through, I would figure it out.

Her magic words actually upset me. I didn't believe in her magic words anymore—rather, I thought it was the magic words that put me into trouble. They were what made me take the risk blindly and didn't prepare me enough for all the struggles I was going through. I tried to figure everything out, and look where that got me.

I said to her, "Then why am I here? Why do you have to work two jobs while finishing college if you can figure out anything?"

With a brief pause, she said, "Because we are in the process of figuring things out, and that is not always pretty."

That, I didn't think about. Ever since I used her magic words, things seemed to fall on my lap. Like when I found my opportunity to come to America through Korean American Student Conference. Like when I only applied to BU and was accepted. Like when I already had a friend whose roommate is leaving soon and didn't even need to find a room for myself. I forgot about the amount of effort I had to put in to actually get to this point and believed that things had to come my way naturally and effortlessly. When things were hard, I was stressed out and thought it shouldn't be this way.

I looked into her eyes and said, "I guess you're right. I'm going through a small bump in the road."

After she left, I went back to my room. Once the doctor told me I had to stay there for at least five days, I stopped fighting. I stopped resisting what was happening in my world. I was just present, coloring in my drawing books and hoping the time would pass. It didn't even annoy me when Sarah knocked on the bathroom every ten minutes to check up on me. When Mark, the guy with mild schizophrenic symptoms across the room, was restrained by the staff, I did not even blink. I just went back to the room and did my activities. There was a strange tranquility once I gave up on the need for control.

On Wednesday, I was released. Then I checked my phone and texted my family I got my phone back.[12] I packed up my belongings and put my shoes on. Coming out of the center,

---

12 I couldn't tell my family what happened; but four years later when I was ready, I brought it up to my sister. She said it made her sad to imagine how hard things were to me back then but was glad things were fine now.

I took an Uber home. In the car, I was looking outside of the window as if it was my first time in the States. Tall trees. Open fields. Old buildings. Diversity. I fell in love with this country before I came here. And my love had not changed. I just forgot about it because I was busy dealing with some new issues I'd never had before.

Soon after relishing my regained freedom, David called to remind me that I had to go to see a therapist on a regular basis. He said he assigned me one closest to my school in Brookline.

The following week, I made my visit to the office for the first time. As I arrived in the area a bit earlier than I needed to, I went into a café to avoid the sun and ordered a cup of coffee. Sitting at the café, I realized the neighborhood looked familiar. I had also been to this café as well. What did I come here for?

Oh, the church.

Several months ago in January, I came to the Korean church in the area. It was a cold morning, and I sat down at this café. That morning, I felt hopeful for the possibility to reconnect with my local Korean community. When I didn't feel I was a part of them, I went back home with a broken heart. If I had continued going to the church, would I have been in this situation today?

I walked into the therapist's office and spent the hour telling her I didn't want the service. As much as the experience had put things into perspective, I didn't trust these people—psychiatrists, psychologists, and therapists. I resented that they made too quick of a judgment to hospitalize me. I was from a different country and had no context around the question of my suicidality.

And that was my first and last visit to her office. When I got back home, I still didn't know why I had running thoughts and withdrew from people. I still didn't know why; as much as I wanted to be happy, I kept walking toward black holes. I didn't come home with an answer—just more resentment and a broken heart.

Several months later, I received $2,000 worth of bills from the center and the ambulance company. My heart sank when I first received the bill, but I remembered things could get messy when I was in the middle of figuring things out. Like my dad taught me back in high school, I tried to focus on what I could control. I spent hours talking with Student Health Services and the companies and explained the situation. They made some kind of arrangement for me, which ended up costing me a lot less than what it was.

Through the experience of figuring things out one by one, the unknown became less scary and more manageable. Then I faced one of the biggest problems that I didn't want to deal with for a long time: my mental health. I knew I was still experiencing anxiety but didn't want to see anyone because of what happened after seeking help. However, I admitted that happened because of a series of unfortunate events. Now that I knew I could call a therapist assigned to me, that shouldn't happen.

By the time I graduated from BU, which was four months after my twenty-fourth birthday, I contacted the therapist David assigned to me. I said I was ready to have a couple of sessions with her.

When I visited her office in Brookline, she welcomed me with open arms. I started opening up about the anxiety and depression symptoms I had been experiencing. Once I spoke my thoughts out loud and shared them with someone else, they became less scary. It felt as if I took out a monster living inside of my body and realized it was missing an arm; it was still scary, but I could fight it.

The therapist asked me questions related to my day-to-day life and social relationships. These questions helped me put things into perspective—I realized I was going through a lot, and anyone in this situation would feel anxious and less confident.

I also asked her questions I was afraid to ask to anybody because they were from the most insecure part of me.

"Do people judge if I live in a rough neighborhood?" I asked her one day after taking a deep breath.

She said, "Some people do, and some people don't."

This simple answer hit me hard; now I knew it wasn't up to me whether I was being judged or not. There was no point of trying not to be judged for who I was because, no matter what, some would judge and others wouldn't.

She also gave me tools to monitor and manage my emotions. For instance, I took notes of the situations that triggered my anxiety and shared with her. Once we saw some patterns, she brainstormed some actions I could take to ease these feelings whenever they occurred, such as removing myself from the situation or taking two minutes to breathe. Knowing my patterns and how to deal with them emboldened me; it taught me I didn't need to stay helpless and be sucked into the black hole.

Slowly but surely, I started learning to do things on my own terms, and growing out of my baby adult phase was such an empowering experience. Now, I could trust that I could learn and figure things out, and like they say, if I could do that in America, I could do it anywhere else.

CHAPTER 8

PERFECT OR NOT

Seeing Forest Beyond the Trees

As a perfectionist, I used to think I have to get everything right. This mindset permeated into something as small as having the exact number of socks when traveling and something as serious as getting all questions right on *Suneung*. My perfectionism kicked in even when I was supposed to relax. When I traveled, I liked to plan out the entire trip in advance, measuring the time taken from one location to another. Like my perfectly planned itinerary, I hoped that my life, work, and relationships all worked out with no shortage or excess.

It's not entirely clear where I picked up this perfectionist mindset, but I know my perfectionism got worse in high school. Because one wrong question on *Suneung* could determine whether I would get accepted to SKY, I studied every concept and solved every problem in the textbooks. Most of the time, I fully understood all the details in the study materials before going into the exam and hoped I get everything right.

Perfectionism helped me excel in life, including the notorious *Suneung* exam because my standards were high. Even at

BU, fanatically paying attention to details led to fairly good results. However, I started noticing that my perfectionism didn't serve me anymore when I started my graduate study in economics at Tufts University in 2018. From the first week of the program, I was swamped with homework, and without a moment to catch my breath, I had to take exams in three weeks after starting the semester.

I remember the moment studying for my first macroeconomics exam in the library, wearing my perfectionist hat and perusing every single word in the materials. While I went through the pile of handouts and the hard-covered textbooks, time flew by. When I thought it only had been an hour, three hours had already passed. I wanted to know everything, but I only had so much time in a day. The day before the test, I only reviewed half of the materials, which I understood the ins and outs of, but I had no idea what was in the other half. Then I started jamming what seemed important in my head, hoping none of these principles showed up on the exam.

My perfectionist way of studying didn't work in graduate school because I had less time and had more things to study. It turned out many of the details I studied were not relevant to the exam. Instead, the exam focused on the key concepts addressed frequently by the professor that were also on practice tests. I missed the forest for the trees. I did worst on this exam compared to any I'd taken in my life.

It's true that seeing the forest requires looking at the trees: To understand big ideas, I have to have enough details. However, I was used to working the other way around; I tried to understand the details first and build the structure from them. One of the reasons why I did this was because I didn't want to miss out on anything important. It was my fear of mistakes that made me obsessed with the nitty-gritty.

After the test, I walked down to the graduate lounge and put away my bag in the locker. Other students started coming into the lounge and talking about the exam. I didn't even want to make a joke about how terribly I did because I felt so embarrassed.

I left the lounge and headed out to the bathroom. I was in line and standing right next to the mirror. I saw how tired I looked. It felt like I was sprinting a marathon. I was running as fast as I could and as long as I could with little break. To save time for showering and resting, I would take a nap in the bathtub, making sure I was only there no more than twenty-five minutes. I started developing muscle twitches on the left side of my face because of too much stress and caffeine.

This is too much, I thought, looking at my reflection.

It was my turn, and I went into the toilet. I had to let out the frustration and anxiety built up in my chest. I knew how lonely it felt to cry in the bathroom, but what else could I do? The bathroom was one of the best places to cry with all the toilet paper within reach, and I could also check myself in the mirror after. I couldn't believe I was crying because I was struggling at school, but there I was.

I came back to the graduate lounge. It seemed like the students stopped talking about the exam and preparing for the next one. I walked up to one of the round tables, where one of my classmates Stephanie was sitting. She moved a bit for me and greeted me, asking how I did on the exam.

"I screwed it up. I couldn't even review the whole materials for the test," I told her.

Stephanie had long brunette hair and light brown eyes, which contrasted with her paper-white skin tone. I could tell she was religious by some of her jewelry. She carried around unusual maturity, strength, and faith. She was calm and articulate, whether we had just gotten out of the exam or had a presentation tomorrow.

"You're not alone. I screwed up that test too," she said.

"You did?" I asked her, surprised.

"Yes, I did." Stephanie shrugged.

Someone as smart as her, who probably got a full-ride scholarship, also screwed up the exam.

"You don't seem that upset, though," I asked her.

"Well, there's nothing I can do about it. Might as well focus on the next exam," she said.

Then she asked me what I was going to do to do better next time.

At that moment, she put me on the spot, but in a good way. She directed my attention to what I can control and figure out my problem. I again realized it took continuous practice to detach from my problem and move on to find a solution.

"I'll have to think about it, but that's a good question," I said.

I went back home and sat on my desk with a pencil and notebook. I thought about why I couldn't review the whole materials and didn't do well on the exam. Apparently, I didn't have enough time, but why was that?

I realized it was my perfectionism that hurt me in an imperfect world with limited resources. It was not only inefficient but also paralyzing. Because I felt pressure to know everything, I was paralyzed even before I started anything. Once I got it started, I focused on less important details until the deadline was right around the corner.

Then I recalled someone once saying, "Done is better than perfect," which I wrote down in my notebook.

But I believed in perfection. That meant there was nothing to add, change, or remove. I loved seeing my work perfectly done. I loved seeing others' perfect work, whether in sports, music, or writing. I loved looking at details and appreciating them. How could I marry these two—the good and bad sides of perfectionism?

After staring at what I wrote, I wrote down another sentence below it.

Done is better than perfect.

Get it done, and make it better.

Getting it done meant I may miss some details here and there, but it had everything that needed to be there. I would then wear my perfectionist hat and refine the details. When I study, for example, I would start from the forest—big ideas, structure, and things the professor spent hours explaining—then use the details to better understand the big picture. Once I was clear on the big picture, I would then look at the extra details.

Now, instead of *getting everything right*, I focused on *making it better*.

It was no longer my fear of mistakes driving me; rather, it was my desire for growth.[13]

This simple shift in mindset led to small but powerful habits. Instead of fixing my eyes on the long-term and perfect results, I decided to set short-term and realistic goals. Instead of cramming after procrastinating, I allocated some time for a smaller goal each day and focused on making things better. Because I had specific goals to work toward, I became more efficient and less paralyzed.

---

13   Psychologists explain these two types of perfectionism as positive or achievement-oriented perfectionism vs. negative or failure-oriented perfectionism. As an example, check out "How to Be the Perfect Perfectionist" by Tho Tsaousides.

A few weeks later, I started preparing for my second macroeconomics exam. I had two weeks left and could spend four hours a day to study for it. I compared the amount of time I had against the amount of the materials—and it was clear I had to go through a chapter every two days.

After setting a smaller goal, I asked myself, *What is the key message of this chapter?* Once I had a clear understanding of what I needed to focus on, I used the details to better understand the key message. Sometimes I met my short-term goal and sometimes I did not, but that was the beauty of setting short-term goals; I was able to stay flexible and adjust my goals on the fly.

By the end of the semester, I became far better at managing my time with better results. Because my "good perfectionism" improved my efficiency, I was able to have a better work-life balance; though I couldn't afford to spend more than twenty-five minutes in the bathtub, I slept at least seven hours a night and exercised. My work was driven by growth, not by my failure, so I was more motivated to celebrate each milestone.

I applied this mindset not only to my study but also to other aspects of life. When preparing for a trip, I allow a wiggle room for pleasant surprises instead of planning everything in advance. When packing for a trip, I understand I may be over- or under-packing and don't spend hours trying to get everything right. At the core of it is the understanding that I may not get everything right, but *I can make it better* if I have to. This approach saved time, effort, and anxiety and added more efficiency and flexibility to my life.

Ironically, I stopped asking myself, *Perfect or not?* Instead, I asked myself whether I showed up today and made it better and if the answer was yes, that was all that mattered.

Graduating from Boston University

3

RECOVERY

CHAPTER 9

FIT IN OR LET IN

Rooted in Myself

———

I'm not good enough.
This thought often occurred to me as I got closer to graduation at BU. I was surrounded by savvy and well-connected students who probably had their next jobs lined up, while I still doubted if I could get a job in America. I wasn't prepared for the real world even if I got all As in economics, authored two research papers, and was even featured by the school magazine.

Why? I couldn't see myself in the world of professionals. It was hard for me to get real-life experience because I was an international student who was getting used to living in America while navigating legal obstacles with my visa. The only experience I had was working for Professor Grace. At her lab, however, I was surrounded by other students rather than experienced professionals. I still didn't know how things worked outside of academia, and I wasn't ready to move on to the next step in my career.

I was also considering graduate school. I discovered my love of research while working for Professor Grace and thought I would be able to gain more professional experience while finishing my graduate study. I applied to a couple of graduate programs by the time I graduated from BU, but there was a gap between my graduation and when I would hear back from those schools.

I ended up graduating from BU without a job. I started to worry if I would have to go back to Korea after all the effort I expended in America. I was desperate to find a job because I wanted to stay here and pay my rent and student loans. I was tired of being broke, still relying on my parents' help, and not being able to give holiday and birthday gifts to people around me. At this point, I just needed a job—really, any job. I even thought about working at a fast-food restaurant, which I would probably not qualify for because I was on a student visa.

I started looking for a data job because I was good at working with computers. I applied for any data-related positions on Indeed, whether they were temporary, contractual, or full time. I was overqualified for most of these jobs, but that was okay—at least these jobs would pay my bills. I also applied to research positions across the United States that would pay salary, but none of them led to interviews.

After a few weeks of searching, I got a call from a hiring agency. They wanted to see whether they should add me to their applicant pool. I was hopeful. It was a good sign; at least something was happening.

On a cold Wednesday morning, I tied my hair low, put my makeup on, and wore a white blouse and black pants. I tried to look as professional as possible because people often said I looked younger than my age. I dropped by Staples to print two copies of my resume. It was another sunny day in winter.

I hopped out of the train and walked to the office, which was in downtown Boston. When I walked into the building, I realized how short I was compared to the high ceilings. This building had shiny marble finishes on the entire floor, and I looked down at my fuzzy reflection. I thought I dressed professionally, trying hard to look at least similar to my age, but it didn't seem to work.

I checked in at the front desk and was directed to the fourth floor. I got on the elevator, which was equally shiny, and pressed the button for four. I felt a knot of anxiety in my stomach and tried to breathe it out, telling myself, *I will be fine. Everything will be fine.*

On the fourth floor, I saw suite number 413. I walked up there and rang the bell. A man in a black suit welcomed me at the door. He seemed to be in his late twenties or early thirties and introduced himself as Allen.

Allen asked me to check in at the front desk. I told my name to the front person again and was seated in the common area. I didn't know what I was supposed to do while I was waiting for an interviewer, so I read—or pretended to read—my resume. After ten minutes or so, another man walked toward me with Allen. He was also wearing a black suit and introduced himself as Joe. We shook hands, and the three of us entered a room and closed the glass door behind us.

I sat at a small round table facing Allen and Joe. They were friendly and tried to make me feel as comfortable as possible with small talk and jokes. Allen introduced himself and his coworker and said they worked with large corporations looking for temporary help, which could become permanent jobs with benefits.

After Allen's introduction, I gave each one a copy of my resume. Joe looked at it and asked,

"You know, a good friend of mine also went to BU. She was in a sorority. Do you remember who the president was?"

I was taken aback by his question. First of all, he assumed I was a part of the sorority. Second, the question had nothing to do with this interview.

"No, I don't. I wasn't in any sorority at BU," I answered.

He nodded and asked again, "Who is the president of BU?"

I gave him the answer but thought these questions were strange.

After a brief pause, Allen opened up.

"Okay. You graduated from BU with a 4.0 GPA in your major. You got magna cum laude in one of the best schools in the US. How is it that you don't have a job yet?"

I got it. They were thinking I was a *scam*. They must be thinking my resume was fake.

I wasn't a scam, of course. There was no single lie on my resume, but I felt like I got caught pretending to be someone else that I was not. I thought, like Joe and Allen, that my resume didn't quite make sense—any normal person who graduated magna cum laude would already have their jobs lined up.

The real story was I came to the States less than two years ago. Getting a full-time job doesn't miraculously happen right out of college. Students have to understand what they can do and what they want, first of all. Then logistics must be figured out, from writing a resume and cover letter to getting prepared for interviews. Even if someone did everything right, competition is intense for entry-level positions, and opportunities are limited for international students.

I gave them a quick and convenient answer even though that was not a full story. I said my visa status as an international student didn't seem to entice many employers. They nodded.

After the interview, they saw me off at the door. Going down to the lobby, Allen's question lingered like a bitter taste.

How is it that you couldn't get a job? The question hit one of the most insecure parts of me. I didn't want to accept the reality, so I didn't want to think about it. But when others saw this part of me, I felt the world found out who I really was. I felt like an imposter.

* * *

While Allen and Joe kept their promise and emailed me job opportunities as they came up, I finally got invited for an interview from a private company. It was a data-entry position at a global supermarket company, and I would be hired as a temporary employee and move up to a full-time position with benefits.

My background, by anyone's standard, was overqualified. The job only required a high school degree, and I would use none of the complicated mathematical and economic concepts I learned at school. But I was okay with it. Considering I had so little experience in the States, I didn't feel like being overqualified. This would be the first step to learn about how things worked at an American organization by doing something less demanding. That was more important to me rather than feeling like an imposter.

The company was in Quincy, a city in south of Boston. When I arrived in Quincy for the interview, I saw a huge building—I think eighteen floors—but it wasn't as intimidating as the ones in Boston. I parked at the nearby garage, walked into the building, and checked in at the front desk. Ten minutes later, a tall woman with a blond bob walked up to me. She introduced herself as Sally. The red frame of her glasses made a nice contrast with her hair color.

After a few questions, she asked me what I did in my free time.

What did I do in my free time? I wondered.

I was a college student taking twenty credits a semester, applying for jobs, and picking up translation projects while working as a research assistant. I didn't have free time. But would that be normal? What if she thought I was someone who pushed myself too hard? Again, I felt the burden of morphing my stories into a "normal" narrative.

What would I do in my free time? I asked myself again. "Read and hang out with friends," I told Sally.

I could tell Sally liked me, but I couldn't shake up the feeling that I wasn't completely honest with her. I pretended to be somebody else even just for small stuff. I didn't even have time to read. I didn't have a lot of friends to hang out with. Why did I make up stuff unnecessarily? Why did I try so hard to sound normal?

I remembered collectivism is predominant in Korea. *We* is often more important than *I*. Thus, being different from a group is considered less desirable—as a popular Korean goes, "A cornered stone meets the mason's chisel." It is common that people follow the majority's decision when their decisions conflict with the majority's. This tendency has its pros and cons: It helps create a more harmonious society, but it can also sacrifice individuals' happiness and freedom. I thought maybe I was conditioned to make myself similar to others so I could avoid "the mason's chisel."

The next day, Sally called me and said I got the job. It paid twenty dollars an hour, which was enough to do what I needed to do. Even if it wasn't entirely aligned with what I wanted, I was happy. I was happy I would start making money with my own skills. I could finally be independent of my parents and even get them nice gifts. I was excited to learn about the real world and how companies worked in America.

I was assigned to a team under the accounting department. Tanya and JK were the first two people I met aside from Sally, and I received training with them. Tanya said she was "Milano" and JK was a white woman. Tanya and JK were friendly and warm. Their clothes were tidy but not too sophisticated. They wore little makeup and flats instead of high heels. They felt like my friends, my neighbors, or some friendly strangers I'd bumped into on a street.

The team had thirteen people and was diverse in terms of ethnicity, education level, gender, and age. Some lived in the outskirts of Boston as I did, but some lived in a suburban neighborhood in Western Massachusetts. Many were American, but one man, Paul, came from Bangladesh. He was the first one in his family to come to the States and spoke English as his second language like me. The youngest one was Ervine, whose parents came from Haiti. He was only twenty-two years old, but his maturity and thoughtfulness shone through him.

Because we were too different, we were all cornered stones, in a sense. Being different was normal and not odd. Differences were interesting, not crazy. It was more frowned upon if you couldn't embrace these differences. The diversity taught me how to be more open to the uniqueness of myself and others, and I slowly became more comfortable with sharing my experiences, thoughts, and judgments even when they were not normal. (What's normal, anyway?)

The American individualism exposed my deep-seated belief that things must be a certain way: I should be a certain way. My career path should be a certain way. My neighborhood should be a certain way. When things were not what they were supposed to be, I wanted to hide parts of who I was. I realized that was the source of me feeling like an imposter who feared the world would find out who she was.

It turned out I was good enough just the way I was. So, I let people in and see my world, which was trying and imperfect. Because my world was good enough as it is, I felt a genuine connection with people. As I saw how important it was to own up to who I was, I made a promise to myself that I would bring my world with me as fully as possible, wherever I go, whether I like all of it or not.

* * *

It was early May in 2018, and I remember everything about this moment. It was a gorgeous springtime in Quincy, and I planned to take a walk after having a delicious chicken pesto sandwich for lunch. After I finished my lunch at the company cafeteria, I checked my inbox on my phone to catch up with personal emails before stepping out. Then I saw an email from Tufts University. I had heard many good things about this school and its economics program. It was a relatively small school and had a beautiful campus.

The email was an acceptance letter. The school also offered me a scholarship covering 80 percent of tuition fees and offering a part-time position as a grader. I remembered I sat at the table with my leftover sandwich, feeling my heart soaring.

Like when I got accepted to Korea University, I called my parents that night. My mom said, "I'm so proud of you," and so did my dad. I told Sally about the news. She was happy about my next chapter and said it had to come.

"Own your story" is a phrase I heard a lot from women I looked up to since I came to America, like Oprah Winfrey. I didn't know what it meant until I started working at this company and met people who seemed comfortable with who they were. To me, owning your story meant I pay attention every time I felt the need to hide or change a part of my world. When this happened, I had to be my own friend, advocate, and guardian to give myself a gentle reminder that this is a part of me, whether I like it or not. This realization was worth a thousand times more than a computer skill.

In August, the school held a luncheon for incoming graduate students and professors. I stepped into a room that had round tables covered with red tablecloths. On one side of the room was a buffet with various kinds of sandwiches and salads.

I remembered attending a similar event at BU, too. The event was for students and parents, and we sat together to talk and learn from each other. I was overwhelmed by the size and people at the event. I wanted to go home, no matter how much I tried to make myself comfortable. I was there with them physically, but I already left the room mentally.

When I saw over twenty graduate students from all over the world and experienced and recognized professors, I sensed that gnawing voice coming back. The voice made me want to leave the room. It made me want to change or hide parts of my story. It made me want to please others. It made me question what I was about to say repeatedly. Like every other life lesson, it was a continuing practice to be okay with feeling like a "cornered stone."

And this gnawing voice asked only one question: *Am I good enough?*

I remembered the promise I made with myself that I would always bring my world fully, whether I like all of it or not. I wouldn't hide or change my stories out of self-doubt. I would not try to fit in, and instead let people in.

I gathered myself and responded to the voice.

Am I good enough to be here? *Yes.*

Am I good enough? *Yes, I am.*

CHAPTER 10

SAFETY NET

Rooted in Us

My safety net has three circles that look like a target. At the core, I have my family, significant other, and besties. These people accept me as who I am (as much as they can at least), and I know I can rely on them.

In the outer circle, I have friendlies. Those are people who I work with, classmates I graduated with, and friends I hang out with occasionally. We know about certain aspects of our lives, but the relationship is not that personal. I don't know if these people would accept me for who I am or if I could rely on them when I'm in trouble. Still, we enjoy each other's company and can give some amount of help when needed.

At the most outer part are people in my communities. I might have never met them, but they are a part of my school, company, Korean communities, and neighborhood. We share a part of our experience and thus can support each other, even though we haven't established personal connections.

Living in a new country taught me how important it was to keep my safety net strong—every part of the circle, from the core to the most outer part. This means putting in the effort to strengthen the relationships as appropriate to each circle. For the core people, I make time to keep them updated with my life and make them feel loved. With friendlies, I check in and spend time together. With my communities, I try to be open, kind, and helpful.

When I first came to the States, I didn't understand the importance of attending to the safety net. It turned out this mistake does more harm than good in America. In a country thousand miles away from home, it was already tricky to make new friends. Many of the local students already had their own social circles, and their weekends were booked with their own friends and family. I had some friends who were also international students, but they tended to go back home or leave to another place to pursue new opportunities. Seeing people come and leave my life, I believed I was better off on my own and my safety net soon wilted.

* * *

Sometimes, you learn the most important lesson through the worst experience you could imagine. Losing someone I loved dearly was the most painful experience I had in life, but it taught me how important it was to attend to my safety net and to care for my loved ones. Because the lesson came with such pain, I never take it for granted.

I grew up with Sia since I was twelve years old. I remembered the day we decided to adopt a dog, and my mom, Yenny, and I went to a nearby adoption center. We saw a palm-sized Shih Tzu devouring his food, who looked back at us with food all around his mouth. Sia had a little brown diamond on his forehead, and my family believed that was the best part to kiss. We loved his curious, playful, and nonchalant personality and welcomed him as a part of our family.

In the first years of becoming our family, he was full of energy and ran everywhere. After several years, he could only walk. Then he started walking more slowly than I did. Sia was there for most of my teenage years, although I couldn't spend much time with him going into high school. But every time I studied, he used to sit next to my chair facing the door. My mom said he was keeping me company and protecting me.

When I left for America, I saw him only once a year. I missed him so much. I missed hugging him, touching him, and going on walks with him. I really loved that my sister created a little social media account dedicated to him, but sometimes, I didn't want to look at the pictures. His pictures reminded me of how far I was from him, and I couldn't do anything to stay close to my baby.

One day during the summer of 2019, my sister posted a picture of Sia when he was a year old. For some reason, I didn't want to look away from his picture. I wanted to look at him closely, even if that hurt me.

Then I left a comment: "I love you, Sia."

I went back home to Korea in early September that year. I made a point of going back to Korea to see my family every year even just for a few weeks. I couldn't wait to hold him in my arms and spend as much time with him as I could. Now that I knew how to drive, I was excited to bring Sia to the beach with my sister. I was also aware that I might not have a lot of time with him. He was fourteen years old, and my mom told me he refused to eat sometimes.

My family picked me up at the airport, and we headed to a restaurant. I was asking my family about my dog, telling them I couldn't wait to see him. I asked my dad, "Do you think he will remember me? What if he doesn't?" to which he assured me, "He remembers you, of course."

After dinner, my mom headed to work, and my sister, Dad, and I came home together. When we arrived in our apartment building, I ran into the elevator. When the elevator stopped on the fifth floor, I pressed "open" multiple times. I ran to our door and put the password in lightning speed. I opened the door quickly and widely, expecting him to wag at the doorstep. But the apartment felt empty. I knew instantly it was missing his scent, his energy, and his presence. I checked every single room to look for him, but he was not there.

I asked my sister and dad, who stood still without saying a word. "He's gone?"

"Come here. I will show you something," said my dad, opening his laptop.

"He's gone," I mumbled, trying to process the situation.

My dad showed me pictures of Sia in a flower basket. He seemed to be asleep. My mom and Yenny were also in the picture looking at Sia in the casket and crying.

"He left when I was here, at least. I woke up and saw him next to me. He left so peacefully that I thought he was asleep."

"When did this happen?"

"On July 16," my sister said.

At that moment, I felt chest pain quickly spreading throughout my body. I felt it every time I breathed, and the pain became my tears. How come I didn't know about this for two months? I resented my family for not telling me earlier, but I also could understand why they did that. What could I do? I was thousands of miles away from home.

I was sick with grief for a week. Everything reminded me of him. The little yellow flowers on his favorite path. The toys he loved. The balcony he liked to sit on and lay down. It was hard to breathe through the pain, and I was exhausted from crying so hard. I was sorry for my baby. I felt sorry for not being able to bring him to the beach, and I felt sorry that all I did was sit down at my desk and study. I felt sorry I lived so far away and couldn't see him as often as I wanted.

My sister said the day I commented on his picture "I love you" was his last day, so he must have heard me saying it. He must have known I loved him dearly.

After two weeks, it was time to come back to Boston. I would never get used to the airport and having to say goodbyes to my family. It was hard every time. When would we see each other again? Next year? Six months later? But it was the life I chose. I decided to go and study on the other side of the earth. The last thing I could do was to tell them how hard it was to leave them behind.

But this time was different. After Sia's passing, I decided to express how much I would miss them and how much I love them. Even though that hurt me. Even though there was nothing I could do. Even though this was the life I chose. Even though that made everyone worried. So, I said, "I wish you guys could come with me," instead of saying, "I'll call you."

My mom said, "Time will wait for us. I promise."

I was worried that expressing my feelings would make everyone sad, but it was the opposite. I felt more supported, loved, and assured.

After settling down at the gate, I thought about how I hadn't known about this for two months. My family members tended to hide worries from each other. And during the summer break, I was losing sleep while looking for an internship and dealing with my own problems. After I got two internships, I was trying to keep things afloat with the weekly stipend of $300. I sent them messages on KakaoTalk, but I didn't call or

FaceTime them because I knew my family would see through to my struggles just from my face. And my family did the same thing. They decided it was best to keep this news from me until I got there. If I ever picked up the phone and called them, I would have known about Sia way earlier.

After I came back to Boston, I started speaking with my family every day. I talked to each of them, whomever was available, and showed them around the campus. I talked to them until I got to the graduate lounge and settled with my coffee. On one of our birthdays, we did a virtual party for each other. Sometimes, I felt like they lived nearby because I talked to them so often. I felt grounded, knowing I came from somewhere and was not alone.

My family was more resilient than I could ever imagine. My parents had two of us in their early twenties while going through some of the worst economic crises in Korean history. My mother changed her job more than five times, from working as a nurse to being a business owner to helping my father pay the bills for the family. My father lived in Dubai for three years with his two young daughters and wife in Korea. They went through a lot, and it would be a pity for me not to tap into their wisdom.

My family, especially Sia, taught me that when we share what is really going on in each other's life, we don't stay worried; we create connections and assure our love for each other. He taught me that my safety net could remind me that I am loved and not alone.

* * *

I believe that people only need one person who accepts them as who they are to learn how to feel secure in their own skin. That one person can remind them they are loved despite their imperfections and mistakes. That one person is someone who we know is more forgiving to ourselves than we are and make us think; maybe we are decent people. This experience of acceptance can become the foundation from which people build confidence and expand themselves to new relationships. To me, Joseph was that person.

I often saw Joseph in the apartment complex I lived in. He came to the complex frequently to take care of a golden retriever of a resident. We first talked to each other at the gym when I asked him where the wipes were. Since then, we bumped into each other and chatted while he was walking the dog, who was impatient to play ball.

By the way he treated the dog and other senior residents in the complex, he seemed like the man with a gold heart. I started looking forward to having conversations with him. I sometimes drove around the complex just to find out whether he was walking the dog. We had a lot to understand about each other as he grew up in America and didn't have much exposure to other cultures, but we also had similarities because we both loved hikes and plants. I especially loved his eyes.

It was in spring when we were getting to know each other. I was close to graduating from Tufts University, worked ten hours a day as a freelance translator, and was applying for full-time jobs. My hair was greasy, and I had breakouts on my face. I was also gaining weight from ramen, especially around my stomach area. If it wasn't for him, I would have no reason to go outside and socialize.

On a Friday afternoon, Joseph knocked on my door and got me out of my apartment. He brought me to a pond nearby that I didn't know existed. The pond stretched far out and had a reflection of the sky. He took pictures of me, and he said I looked beautiful even though that was not what I saw.

He accepted me as who I was and kept reminding me how strong and beautiful despite me not believing it.

He continued to remind me that whatever I was going through, I would find a way out. Even though I didn't feel beautiful and felt uncomfortable in my own skin around this time, his words started brushing up on me. Seeing myself accepted by him, I learned to see my imperfections. I realized they weren't that bad, and I learned to look at my imperfections with compassionate eyes—my clumsiness, my worries, and my awkwardness. His acceptance helped me accept who I was—all parts of my body, my past, and myself.

* * *

He quickly joined the core of my safety net and empowered me through many obstacles in life. One major struggle I had at that time was friendship. He noticed I barely had close friends and asked me why. I said I didn't want to deal with complex relationships when I was already happy on my own. Then he encouraged me to go out and make new friends. His innocent suggestion triggered me, however, because it reminded me of my failed friendship with Eli.

Eli, of course, was at the core of my safety net. But I always felt like a burden to her. There was a power imbalance between us that caused friction and stopped the friendship from thriving. As an international student, I wasn't capable of many things and needed her help more than she needed mine. I didn't know how to drive, I didn't have a car, I just moved to this country, and I had no place of my own. She had a lot more friends and birthday parties than I did.

This power imbalance manifested when she left for a business school in California in 2018. Both of us tried to keep the friendship together, but we drifted apart.

Thinking about Eli, I told Joseph there was no reason to pursue a close friendship. At the time, I was already happy on my own with my family, him, and my old friends from Korea.

Joseph said that might make me *happy*, but it's not *healthy*.

Then it struck me that he might be right. Deep down, I loved people. Picking a birthday gift for people was one of my favorite things to do. It's just that I stopped caring because I was disappointed by people who came and left my life. The reality was I struggled more than I needed without people; if I had a close friend to talk to on my twenty-fourth birthday, I wouldn't have found myself in the behavioral center.

I did want to give it another try.

I didn't know where I should go to make new friends, and Joseph brainstormed with me. I joined a hiking group on Meetup and started saying hi to my neighbors. I had lunch with people I worked with and caught up with my old friends from Korea and America—Dan, Ava, Chelsea, and other people who shared a part of their experience with me. I started opening up more to new people, trying to treat them in the way I wanted to be treated—accepting, reliable, and supportive.

I had to let go of some relationships that were not beneficial to either person. I was still learning how to be a better communicator and supportive friend. But I became better at setting up a healthy boundary for myself and others, and quite a few people quickly came into my safety net. I learned about their worlds, which expanded my worldview. We experienced the world together and exchanged support when we needed it. My life with these people truly became richer, safer, and more enjoyable.

As my safety net became solidified, I started paying attention to my communities such as my graduate school. When some of them had a problem, I helped in any way I could. When I had a problem, they were there to think through the problem together. Even though we might not have deep personal connections one on one, we could offer support to each other because we were sharing a part of our lives.

I call my network of people "the safety net" because they are the ones with whom I can exchange support—whether for emotional or tangible support. They are the foundation for me to show up in a new environment as who I am and to pursue new opportunities despite the unknown. As someone living in a new environment, I learned it was essential to put effort to keep this net clean and strong. Hopefully, one day, I can become that person who can remind people they are accepted and loved unconditionally.

One night, I picked up the phone and texted Eli. Now that I had learned more about relationships, I realized it was my own insecurity that drove us apart. In the end, it didn't matter which one of us got more help. That's how we grew and learned together. After exchanging some words, I told her, "Hey, I miss you. You were like a gift to me. Hope we could see each other when you come to the East Coast."

CHAPTER 11

REAL OPTIMISM

Rooted in Truth

Ever since I achieved my goal of going to SKY, I wanted to believe that everything would all work out in my favor. My optimism grew stronger when I met Eli, who taught me the power of magic words, "We'll find a way." My optimism motivated me to take on big risks and to step out of my comfort zone with little hesitation. A lot of things did work out in my favor, and I believe my optimism deserves credits for them.

The problem was I had what psychologists called optimism bias. When people have optimism bias, they overestimate the likelihood of positive events and underestimate the risks of negative events. For instance, many smokers tend to underestimate the possibility of contracting lung cancer, and married couples downplay their chance of getting divorced. In my case, I didn't think through the challenges I would face after moving to the United States. Researchers like Tali Sharot show that most of us are the victims of optimism bias.

Because I came to the States without being prepared for negative events, I didn't know how to deal with them.

Whenever they happened to me, I just relied more on my optimism and went through a host of trials and errors more than what was necessary. When I rescued myself from a crisis, I thought, *See? Everything would eventually work out.* I then went back to my optimism without thinking about what I could do to be more prepared in the future; to me, having a plan B meant I doubted the power of my optimism.

So, life decided to throw me a big reality check, much bigger than everything I went through for the past five years.

It was March 2020, and I was getting close to graduating from Tufts University after two years of relentless work. I really hoped my parents could make it to my graduation ceremony this time. I knew it was hard for them to take time off from for over a week to fly all the way to America. But I wanted to celebrate it with my family—the people I love, the people I could rely on.

I brought up this idea to my parents when I visited Korea in December 2019, and surprisingly, I got their yes. They also felt like it was the time to see where their daughter had lived for five years. My mom had never traveled overseas, and my dad had never been to the US. My sister and I were giggling, talking about how funny it would be to see our parents in the middle of Manhattan because we couldn't imagine their reactions. Would they be overwhelmed? Would they be excited? The next day, the family booked round-trip tickets for May 2020.

Soon after getting the promise from my parents, I left Korea to finish up my last semester. My sister took a gap year after graduating from college and came to stay in America for a couple of months. We made a stop in Paris for five days, which became one of the most memorable trips I ever had. We explored bakeries, walked along the Seine River, and took pictures of each other at the Louvre. Making up for the lost time with my sister, I couldn't have been any happier.

Around this time, though, I was hearing about a novel virus spreading in China. I saw people starting to wear masks in Korea, but I didn't think it could travel all the way to America. Even though it somehow came here, I didn't imagine it could spread so quickly because America was not as dense as Korea or China.

I was completely wrong about that.

When the country went into a lockdown in March 2020, my roommate Diana did what was best for her, like everyone else at that time. Her family lived in Nevada, and it didn't make sense for her to stay in Massachusetts and deal with the uncertainty without them. At her home, she could stay close to her parents and grandparents and worry less about her grocery bills, while having enough toilet paper and saving money on rent. She brought up one night that she'd like to leave and hoped I would understand. It was obvious that her decision would have financial consequences on my end, but I also didn't want to stop her doing what was best for her.

When she left, I had to take over our once-shared bills that amounted to $2,600 a month. My only sources of income were my student loans and the graduate teaching assistantship, which paid me $800 every other week. I could not afford to break the lease, nor did I have anywhere else to go. I stayed in my two-bedroom apartment with my sister, hoping I would get a job right after graduation and find my way out.

I was getting closer and closer to my graduation. No one knew how the pandemic would affect the job search for recent graduates. People said things would be difficult because companies wouldn't have time to hire new people, but others said this was an opportunity to find a remote job.

For international students, the unpredictable job market only added more uncertainty because most of them only had three months after graduation to find a job. It worsened my disappointment that the school canceled the graduation ceremony my family had looked forward to.

Despite my prayers and efforts, I graduated without a job like I did when I graduated from BU. I really didn't feel like celebrating the graduation; I didn't think I had anything to celebrate. My future was full of unknowns: I didn't know where I would be going next. I wasn't sure whether I could get a job in America. I didn't know if I could pay the bills. All I could think about was that I was going through one of the worst possible post-graduation periods.

But my sister insisted. She told me, "We are celebrating the efforts you put in for the past two years. It is already a big achievement to finish a graduate program in America." She got a small strawberry cake and set up graduation balloons in the kitchen. She prepared salmon and garlic shrimp. She filmed a video of our little party and sent it to my parents, who were still disappointed about the canceled trip.

After the celebration, I said goodnight to my sister and went back to my room. I laid down on my bed and remembered Stephanie, who I met at Tufts University. Right before the school went remote, we headed to the library together and talked about our next steps after graduation. We both didn't have what we wanted yet. She seemed stressed out, and for the first time, doubted herself. I wanted to bring her strength back, so I told her, "Hey! Let's not worry too much. We will find a way."

To that, she took a deep breath, put on a smile, and told me, "I know. We will figure it out."

Stephanie helped me to figure out my academic struggles by directing my attention to what I can control. Remembering

Stephanie and her wisdom, I decided to focus on what I can control. In this situation, all I could do is to keep doing what I was doing. I gave myself a date of July 30, which was two months from my graduation. Before July 30, I would put my head down and do everything I could do to get myself out of the situation. I wouldn't think about how scared and worried I was. I wouldn't blame anyone else. I would keep trying and moving on.

I started working as a freelance translator seven days a week while applying for jobs full time. I visited the career center every week and met with my career coach. I reached out to other graduate students to see their resumes and cover letters. I asked for advice from recent graduates who got their dream jobs. They really went the extra mile to get their jobs; one of them even had a spreadsheet of more than a hundred companies they applied to.

I started seeing what I could improve and worked tirelessly to bring myself up to the standards. I was learning every day, hoping all these efforts could get me my dream job, which was to work at an international organization.

It was June 30, and I didn't get any callbacks. I was running out of money and couldn't afford to live in my apartment. The landlord kept telling me I should renew my lease soon and give her ninety days' notice in advance. My sister was leaving as well, so I would be left on my own.

It was rock bottom. I would probably have given up if it wasn't the July 30 date I set for myself. (Then again, I didn't have any other options to fall back on if I gave up on this.)

Sitting down on my bed that night, mentally and physically exhausted, I thought about my first flight coming to the States, looking around at other Koreans at the airport and thinking whether things were really better in America.

I remembered ignoring a knot of anxiety in my stomach because I didn't want to believe I could be wrong. Now the reality was I did not have the career of my dreams and didn't have any better of a life in the US.

Then I took a deep breath, remembering that I am good enough no matter what. Even if this dream job doesn't happen, I am good enough. Even if I screw things up here, I at least tried, so that's good enough. The reality is it is a big deal to get hired by these international organizations; many people around the world want to work for them. So, it would be quite alright if I don't get it because I can do something else to empower people with whatever I have, wherever I am.

It would be alright, no matter what.

Once I faced the reality, I felt liberated from the burden I had imposed on myself for so many years. I let go of my obsession with my dream job, dream life. Then I started seeing more paths and possibilities in the future and felt less scared of the uncertainty. For the first time after graduation, I slept well.

Going into early July, I was printing out job descriptions and updating my resume as usual. A stack of documents was already beside me, and I remembered staring at them as the pile got higher and higher. At this point, I felt more determined than exhausted; I was determined to cross the finish line, whatever happened.

Then I checked my email mindlessly, and it said, "Interview Request for Yujin Kim." It was from the employer I've been wanting to work for a long time. I gasped loudly, and it took me about an hour to calm myself down. I responded to the email, overthinking every word I was writing. The next day, I got another interview request from the same employer but a different department.

It was a strange experience how, even before the first interview, I cried out of joy and relief. After that, I got through the four stages of the hiring process with strange calmness. A few weeks later, they told me four hundred people applied for this one position, and I was the one they selected.

From this experience, I learned that Eli's magic words, "You'll find a way," were missing something very important. It was the attitude of seeing the reality as it is, whether I like it or not. In my case, I needed to keep learning about the job search process and accept that I couldn't hold onto the hope for my dream job when I couldn't even pay my bills at that moment. Once I understood this, her magic words became clearer: Understand the reality, *then* you'll find a way.

* * *

I booked a tour for several apartments and drove down to DC, which took me eight hours. I hated saying goodbye to people I met in Boston. But I was excited about my next chapter, a fresh start.

After eight hours of driving, I passed the border of Delaware and Maryland and finally got to the DC area when the sun set. It was a humid yet beautiful summer day in DC. Before checking in my hotel, I got some Japanese ramen to go and spent the first night in Holiday Inn around the University of Maryland. I knew that from here on, my place was how I wanted it to be. I was excited, grateful, and relieved.

The apartment hunting was successful. I got a small apartment in a nearby neighborhood, which had all that I needed and wanted: a clean interior, a dishwasher, an in-unit laundry, and a dryer... I came back to Massachusetts to start preparing for the move. Since I was living in a two-bedroom apartment, I had to throw away and sell a lot of things. I was especially attached to my furniture—the dining table I ate and studied on, my vanity, and my little desk. It was hard to let them go, but they soon found their owners. Some man, who picked up the vanity for his daughter, sent me a picture of her reading a book beside the vanity. Another one came for the desk with their children, who needed a new place to work from home. I had to say goodbye, but at least they found their new, little owners.

After moving to my new apartment, I often reflected on my past. Now that I had settled down in America, I thought about which of my mindset helped or didn't help me. Especially, I questioned why I felt so much calmer when I let go of my optimism—when I thought maybe this dream job won't happen for me.

The book that gave me an answer to this question was *Good to Great* by Jim Collins. I bumped into this book at a library and remembered seeing it on Professor Grace's shelf. I borrowed the book and started reading it that night.

The book was about what sets apart the leaders who brought a company in a crisis to success. One of the characteristics is what Jim Collins called "the Stockdale Paradox," which was inspired by the story of James Stockdale. He was a prisoner of war in the Hỏa Lò Prison, the infamous "Hanoi Hilton" in North Vietnam, for eight years from 1965 to 1973 as a senior naval officer.

What Stockdale went through was beyond horror. The captors tortured and interrogated him repeatedly, and Stockdale's leg was broken twice. Nevertheless, he showed determination for nonconformity. He, for instance, injured himself multiple times with a stool and a razor, so the captives couldn't use him as an example of a "well-treated prisoner." His invincible spirit discouraged the captives and stopped them from using excessive torture toward all prisoners of war. In February 1973, he was released from prison and returned to the US.

Collins asked Stockdale how he was able to withstand these uncertain and painful times. Stockdale answered, "You must never confuse faith that you will prevail in the end—which you can never afford to lose—with the discipline to confront the brutal facts of your current reality, whatever they might be."

In other words, people need faith to forge their futures *and* discipline to assess their reality.

To Stockdale, optimists often didn't have the discipline to assess reality. These optimists believed they would be released by a specific date, such as the next Thanksgiving or Christmas. When the date arrived and things didn't change, these optimists perished from disappointment. They, like me, were the ones who underestimated the chance of bad news and didn't mentally prepare themselves.

Stockdale's mentality is close to what psychologists call realistic optimism. As Collins noted, this optimism is one of the key factors to resilience and is found in many company leaders who rescued their companies from a crisis.

I was the "optimist" in many areas of life that Stockdale talked about—I believed my wishes were coming true without examining the reality surrounding them, and any obstacles would go away miraculously. Once I faced my obstacles and weaknesses, however, I was on the path to assess my reality and find a way out, *really*.

This concept of realistic optimism was what motivated me to write my first book. I was fascinated by this concept and listened to podcasts and read books on this topic. I interviewed counselors, psychologists, and people who achieved their goals and found out they all in some way had this mindset. I figured this all out on my own, but I really started to notice significant improvement once I felt bolstered by other voices. I wanted to join the efforts to spread this mindset for whoever going through changes and uncertainty in their lives by sharing my experience.

* * *

After a year of starting my job, I signed up to be a mentor for international students. I had three mentees, who are all international students and attend Tufts University as graduate students.

I remembered one of my mentees asked for advice before leaving for the US. On our virtual call, I could see through the excitement she was having about the future in America. She, like me, couldn't wait to learn and grow in the bigger world and wondered how she could make the best out of her time.

Her enthusiasm reminded me of my past self, who was so excited about studying in America. Granted, she was doing better than me because she actively sought out advice from someone experienced. What did I need to hear the most at the beginning?

"Not to kill your excitement but..." I opened up about my experiences—good and bad. I told her people experience many challenges in America that could take a serious emotional toll in a way she never experienced before. It's important for her to be aware of and be prepared for them, so when that happens, she wouldn't be caught off guard. I cautioned her to talk to some other people besides me who experienced and overcame their challenges. Hard times might pass by more quickly than imaginable, and she'd be able to enjoy what America could offer to its fullest.

She thanked me for my advice, and I wished her the best.

And this was the type of optimist I became.

The one who always looks up, but the one who is acutely aware of her limitations.

The one who works tirelessly for what she wants, but the one who can also let go.

The one who believes she will be alright in the end, no matter what.

Sia

Mom and Dad

My sister and me

4

MASTERY

CHAPTER 12

RENEWED

Would I Still Come to America?

One of my favorite trails in Massachusetts is Lynn Woods, where I can look over the skyline of Boston. The last time Joseph and I went there was in April 2021, when the spring breeze gently brushed my face. The spring breeze in the cold evoked some emotions; I felt relieved yet sad. I felt nostalgia, but it was stained with pain.

Looking at the Boston skyline, I started to think about my four years as an international student in America. As soon as I arrived in this country, all my achievements in Korea felt insignificant because people didn't know about them. I pushed myself too hard to restore what I had, and the pressure broke a part of me. Language and cultural roadblocks crumbled my self-esteem. Living with a sense of otherness, I tried to morph my stories into something normal and cut out the things that looked different and ugly. I barely had close relationships and spent my birthdays and holidays alone. On top of all these challenges, I was still worried about how long I could stay in the US.

Then I asked myself, *Would I still come to America if I knew how it would be?*

Many of my struggles arose naturally because I moved to a new environment. Like a Korean saying goes, even trees get ill for three years when they are moved to a new land. But some trees fare better than others. The ones who endure the wind, rain, and storm have strong and web-like roots that firmly grasp the ground. And that was what I lacked. The strength to hold the ground, regardless of what was going on above it. The resilience to support myself in the face of setbacks without trauma.

Over the years, I learned to keep my root in three places—in myself, in my safety net, and in truth. Like trees that firmly put down their roots, I am able to endure bad storms because I am rooted in these three places.

I am rooted in who I am by owning my identity in its entirety, whether it is pretty or not. My experience matters to me, even if it doesn't matter to others. Instead of fitting in with others, I let people into my world.

I am rooted in my safety net, the people with who I can exchange love and support. I am assured that I have people to fall back on, ask for guidance, and share my disappointment and victory. Because we have each other, we can fly high, together.

I am rooted in the truth by accepting the reality as is, whether I like it or not. I understand that what I want may not happen but do not lose faith that something better is on its way.

Still now, I have moments when I want to pull back, doubt myself, and get carried away overthinking about the future. But my past has trained me to pick up myself quickly and not allow myself to fall.

Looking over the skyline, I was thinking, despite all its imperfections, I like this country. Actually, I am in love with this country. More than I was before I came here, hearing Hannah's stories about big houses and big lands. More than I was when I first came here and was awestruck in the middle of Manhattan. I love the individuality, diversity, and creativity that America offers. There may be a lot of drama and opinions, but that also means people are free to speak their minds, which is not possible in many parts of the world. I like how down to earth and family-oriented many people are. I like the proximity to nature even in big cities. Most of all, I saw how America dealt with some of the toughest problems and found solutions. To me, despite all the ups and downs, America is resilient, and I admire it.

In the end, America gave me what I asked for—freedom and opportunities. I have the freedom to define my path and to speak my mind. I work in the industry of my dream and meet people from all around the world, who are smart, hardworking, and generous. I am privileged to do what I do and earn the income that fulfills my needs and wants.

But most importantly, yet unexpectedly, I received a gift called resilience. Resilience may not be pretty because it is a byproduct of striving for the better, every single day and throughout the ups and downs. Yet it is a beautiful gift because it is not about the fights and struggles, but it is about hopes and dreams.

Leaving behind the view, we began walking down to the trail. As far as I could see, I am planning to settle down in America. I hope my career continues to bloom so I can also contribute back to my home country. I want to start a family here; I will do my best to teach Korean and feed Korean food to my future half-Korean children.

Now, it was clear what my emotions were telling me. All of them—relief, sadness, nostalgia, and pain—coexisted, amalgamated into one emotion. And that was *gratitude*.

If I would have to do it all over again, I would.

I would still come to America.

Celebrating my twenty-eighth birthday in DC

A BRIEF GUIDE ON BECOMING SURE

For the readers who may experience similar difficulties as I had, I want to summarize the mental health challenges I presented in the memoir and how I overcame them. Studies found these challenges are common among international students or people moving to a new country, so hopefully, my tips are useful for you.

Note: These problems can be born out of systematic reasons beyond our control. Here, I focus on what we can control so we can do our part in overcoming these difficulties. I believe once we do our part, it will become easier to see where the root problem lies and make consorted efforts to solve the problem on a higher level as necessary.

In *Part II. A Bump on the Road*, I present five mental health challenges and tips:

1. **Language and communication insecurity**: Remember you didn't grow up in America, but make continuous efforts to improve your language and communication

skills. It takes time to become fluent in English if it is not your mother tongue. It takes time to understand communication norms such as being to the point, having small talk, making direct eye contact, and respecting personal space. With these points in mind, working on your language and communication skills will help you feel surer of how you communicate with others.

2. **Feeling of otherness**: Withhold your assumptions about others and look for shared experiences. Diversity in America can make differences more visible than our similarities. Because of these perceived differences, you may be unconsciously making assumptions about others. For instance, when I went to the Korean church, I assumed I would not get along with others because we are likely to have different socioeconomic backgrounds. The thing is we can always find shared experiences that could connect us beyond our differences. This helped me ease the pressure of fitting into a group, and I became more confident and surer about who I am.

3. **Stereotyping**: We cannot change others' behaviors, but we can do our part by seeing people as individuals beyond their group identity. Notice the stereotypes you may be imposing on yourself or others, then it becomes easier to see what others impose on you. Don't be afraid of pointing out when others display stereotypical behavior toward you, as appropriate to the situation. However, if bias becomes discrimination or violent racism, I suggest reporting the incident to the school authority. Do your research on the resources available at your school. Boston University, for example, has a

guideline for reporting these incidents in confidence by contacting the Equal Opportunity Office or the Dean of Students Office. The school may also provide counseling services you could tap into.

4. **Feeling or being incompetent ("a baby adult")**: Focus on what you can control, and figure it out. It is true that many things may be out of your control as an international student, so start by clarifying what you can control. Then do some serious research, on- and offline, about the step to solve your problem. I tend to talk to the people I trust first and gather information, then take the necessary steps. Whichever approach you take will depend on the situation, but figuring things out is an inevitable part of living in a new country. As you gain more experience in tackling your problems, the unknown will become less scary and more manageable.

5. **Perfectionism**: Adopt growth-oriented perfectionism instead of failure-oriented perfectionism. With failure-oriented perfectionism, I had an abstract "perfect result" in mind and focused on not making errors to live up to that standard. This often resulted in paying too much attention to unnecessary details, procrastinating, and anxiety. Growth-oriented perfectionism requires us to divide a task into realistic and measurable milestones. It directs our attention to showing up and consistently improving what we built yesterday. Remember the last time you looked back on a situation and said, "That was perfect." Didn't that happen when you allowed some wiggle room and spontaneity instead of planning everything out in advance? This approach

is nimble and efficient, allowing us to feel more certain about each step we're taking.

In *Part III. Recovery*, I present three broad pieces of advice on managing self-doubt and feeling sure as a newcomer. I still check in with myself on these three things whenever I face emotional and practical difficulties.

1. **Owning who I am ("rooted in myself")**: Most of my problems eventually come from one source: self-doubt. Embrace and share your path, experience, and strengths/weaknesses even if they are not considered normal. For example, when I worked at an American company, I was only Korean in that place. I didn't have the excitement around football seasons but shared it as is, even though it was not normal in where I was. Once you choose to show up as who you are, you will feel a lot more confident in your skin, which in my case led to more genuine relationships with others.

2. **Attending to my social safety net ("rooted in us")**: Keep in touch with your loved ones back home while building new relationships in America. This is not to say you should attend five parties a week and have a few thousand followers on social media. The key is to find and maintain supportive relationships, who you can exchange emotional and tangible support. You could start from your own communities such as religious groups or ethnic student clubs and expand your relationships with people from different walks of life.

3. **Having realistic optimism ("rooted in truth")**: Stay as close to the truth as possible while having a positive outlook for the future. To me, anxiety arises when I am fuzzy about my goal or problem. I talk to different people and do thorough research to understand that thing giving me anxiety. Knowledge about my reality empowers me because now I can make informed decisions as to what to do.

If you think these problems impact you and your relationships, consider speaking with a school counselor. They may not have the same experience as you, but they can provide useful skills to help you cope with the challenges you are experiencing. (Remember my stories from "Baby Adults"! Unless it is truly what you're going through, be mindful of expressing your emotions using words with intent to harm yourself or others.)

Hope this insight helps.

With love,
Yujin

APPENDIX

INTRODUCTION

Institute of International Education. "Enrollment Trends." *OpenDoorsData*. Accessed January 15, 2022. https://opendoorsdata.org/data/international-students/enrollment-trends/.

Kirmayer, Laurence J., Lavanya Narasiah, Marie Munoz, Meb Rashid, Andrew G. Ryder, Jaswant Guzder, Ghayda Hassan, Cécile Rousseau, and Kevin Pottie. "Common Mental Health Problems in Immigrants and Refugees: General Approach in Primary Care." *Canadian Medical Association Journal* 183, no. 12 (September 2011): E959–E967. https://www.cmaj.ca/content/183/12/E959.

Lysgaard, Sverre. "Adjustment in a Foreign Society: Norwegian Fulbright Grantees Visiting the United States." *International Social Science Bulletin* 7 (1955): 45–51. https://psycnet.apa.org/record/1956-00871-001.

Okai, Lawrencia Baaba. "International Students' Adjustment Challenges in the United States: A Case Study of West Virginia University." (PhD diss., West Virginia University, 2020). 7974. https://researchrepository.wvu.edu/etd/7974.

Park, Hyejoon, Meng-Jung Lee, Ga-Young Choi, and Janet S. Zepernick. "Challenges and Coping Strategies of East Asian Graduate Students in the United States." *International Social Work* 60, no. 3 (July 2016): 733–749. https://journals.sagepub.com/doi/abs/10.1177/0020872816655864?journalCode=iswb.

CHAPTER 1 LONGING

Han, Jane. "LA Targets Korean 'Birth Tourists'." *The Korean Times*, February 4, 2013. http://koreatimes.co.kr/www/news/opinon/2013/02/137_130010.html.

Korean Council for University Education. *The Basics of University Admissions for the 2023 Academic Year.* Seoul, Korea: 2020. Accessed February 15, 2022. https://docviewer.nanet.go.kr/reader/viewer.

CHAPTER 2 SKY

Ock, Hyun-ju. "Blind Hiring System to be Implemented in Public Sector." *The Korean Herald*, July 5, 2017. http://www.koreaherald.com/view.php?ud=20170705000768.

CHAPTER 6 SECRET BOX

World Population Review. "South Korea - General Info."
Accessed February 10, 2022.
https://worldpopulationreview.com/countries/south-korea-population.

CHAPTER 8 PERFECT OR NOT

Tsaousides, Theo. "How to Be the Perfect Perfectionist."
Psychology Today (blog). May 6, 2016.
https://www.psychologytoday.com/us/blog/smashing-the-brainblocks/201605/how-be-the-perfect-perfectionist.

CHAPTER 11 REAL OPTIMISM

Collins, Jim. *Good to Great.* New York City: HarperCollins, 2001.
Sharot, Tali. "The Optimism Bias." *Current Biology* 21,
    Issue 23 (December 2011): R941–R945.
    https://doi.org/10.1016/j.cub.2011.10.030.
UMass Lowell. "Optional Practical Training (OPT)
    Frequently Asked Questions." Accessed February 18, 2022.
    https://www.uml.edu/isso/opt/faq.aspx.

A BRIEF GUIDE ON BECOMING SURE

Boston University Equal Opportunity Office. "Complaint
    Procedures in Cases of Alleged Unlawful
    Discrimination or Harassment." February 2015.
    https://www.bu.edu/eoo/equal-opportunity-affirmative-action/complaint-procedures-in-cases-of-alleged-unlawful-discrimination-or-harassment/.

Lysgaard, Sverre. "Adjustment in a Foreign Society: Norwegian Fulbright Grantees Visiting the United States." *International Social Science Bulletin* 7 (1955): 45–51. https://psycnet.apa.org/record/1956-00871-001.

Okai, Lawrencia Baaba. "International Students' Adjustment Challenges in the United States: A Case Study of West Virginia University." (PhD diss., West Virginia University, 2020). 7974. https://researchrepository.wvu.edu/etd/7974.

Park, Hyejoon, Meng-Jung Lee, Ga-Young Choi, and Janet S. Zepernick. "Challenges and Coping Strategies of East Asian Graduate Students in the United States." *International Social Work* 60, no. 3 (July 2016): 733–749. https://journals.sagepub.com/doi/abs/10.1177/0020872816655864?journalCode=iswb.

ACKNOWLEDGMENTS

I am indebted to my family, significant other, and friends for their support and encouragement throughout the ups and downs of my two-year publishing journey. I am deeply thankful to my 136 supporters for believing in my book early on and showing me incredible generosity and kindness.[14] Without them, this book wouldn't have been possible.

For your kindness, time, and feedback, I am grateful to my beta readers Toni Apatira, Patrick Greenwood, and Sruti Vijaykumar. I thank the twenty-two interviewees who generously shared their experience and wisdom: Matt Casey, Jacob Chuslo, Jennifer Davis, Khaled Eltokhy, Anika Gupta, Girish Harinath, Jieun Hong, Paul Koppenhaver, Chris Loper, Shana Merrifield, Ashley Miller, Alfredo Montufar-Helu, Justin Nguyen, Bao Nguyen, Qiuyun Shang, Raimy Shin, Neha Shukla, Grace Talusan, Honson Tran, Dr. Jeffrey Zabel, Kai Zhang, and Jason Zhang.

For your help on spreading the words, my gratitude goes to Liz D'Amelio and Sarah Fardeen from the International Mental Health Association, Hyun Young Joo and Micheal

---

14 Their names are included at the end of this section.

Blair from the NOVA Korean Language Exchange Group, the WB-IMF Korean Staff Association, the IMF RARO Committee, the DMV Asian Social Group, the Mustard Seed Generation, and Amanda Chin from Study International.

Last but not least, I thank the New Degree Press team for guidance, editorial support, and publishing assistance. A special thank you to Professor Eric Koester for sharing his knowledge in book writing and publishing and to Marketing and Revision Editor Whitney McGruder, Development Editor Quinn Karrenbauer, and Copy Editor Emily Kim for bringing out the best out of my memoir.

Thank you all for making my first book possible. I am blessed and grateful.

Patrick Greenwood
Vincent Clavette
방혜정 (Hyejung Bang)
Anthony Seruwagi
Paul Lee
Christina Oh
Daniel Lee
Khaled ElTokhy
Marian Lobell
Qiuyun Shang
Mai Tong Vang
Tianyuan Wang
Michelle Lam
Jingzhi Liu
Darrell Kilpatrick
Alicia P.
Rose Aruta
Edbert Jao
Doris Sew Hoy
Yesle Kim
Jie Zhou
Neha Shukla
Mohamed Diaby
Guangqi Li
Sophie Wu
Mohammad Ahmad
Ryan Yost
Toni Apatira
Honson Tran
김동찬 (Dongchan Kim)
Adam Siddiq
Wil Cardwell
Von Gerik
Saneg Hun
Yarou Xu
Michael Brown
Tiffany Xiong
Hannah Koh
Giorgianna Ellis
Kara Dischinger
Jonathan Tang
Trinh Vu
Eslem Imamoglu
Yna Divinagracia
Anthony Cruz
Chloe Kim

Fernanda Douglas
Sheng Qu
Nate Vernon
Mitesha S. Shakya
Ashley Galloway
Charlotte Sebin Kim
Myeongju Yoon
Prachi Patki
Mahmut Kutlukaya
김예원 (Yewon Kim)
Joseph Zhang
방성욱 (Seongwook Bang)
Austin Knightly
Nam Thai-tang
Manu Peethambar
Kianna Mckenzie
Yome Nguyen
Crystal Fernandes
Madeline Fink
Yuou Wu
Kazuki Motohashi
Wenya Yan
Shan Lu
Khamal Clayton
Nayun Eom
Nianci Lyu
Jae Seong Lee
Maria Motta
Kaj Luu
Jieun Kim
Yuxian Chen
Julieta Ladronis
Sruti Vijaykumar
Michelle Veth
Sanjana Pradhan
Jinyoung Kim
Shaunak Pagnis
Chang Huh
Layheab Ly
Hlee Yang
Jang Sang Hyun
Kanika S. Mam
Paul Koppenhaver
Emma Karrenbauer
Liat M. Shapiro
Kaiwen Guo

Yukiko Nakayama
Dustin A. Smith
LaNysha Adams
Jaehyung Jang
Riki Matsumoto
Ashley Lam
Jieun Hong
Cindy Kang
Emily Reum
Lahir Marni
Frank Liu
Nurhan Guner
Christy Borja
世托 孙 (Shituo Sun)
Sean Kim
Siddhi Shah
Thomas Le
Kezhou Miao
Khadijah Khogeer
Jeeyeonie
Ariel Huynh
Vanny Neov
Danielle Ferrer
Michael Blair
Shreya Somani
Robert Lee
Eric Koester
Christine Engelhardt
Qihao Tang
Virat Singh
Hyunna J. Nam
Zoeanne Juang
Monica Brova
Natalia Sabater
Esra U. Kutlukaya
Hui Min Tang
Eunnare Sung
Kwesi K. Arhin
Da Yeon Seo
Damilola Apatira
Vatsal Nahata
Matthew S. Casey
Dae Hyeon Jeong
Arol Thamba
George Huang
Sanghyeok Kim

www.ingramcontent.com/pod-product-compliance
Lightning Source LLC
LaVergne TN
LVHW010329070526
838199LV00065B/5698